Live Bait

MINNETONKA, MINNESOTA

Fishing author Dick Sternberg often turns to live bait, and considers it a key component of his angling arsenal.

Live Bait

Mike Vail
Vice President,
Product and Business Development

Tom Carpenter
Director of Book and New Media Development

Dan Kennedy
Book Production Manager

Jenya Prosmitsky
Book Design & Production

Gina Germ
Photo Editor

Michele Teigen
Book Development Coordinator

Janice Cauley
Proofreading

Brook Martin
Bait Wrangler

Principle Photography
Bill Lindner Photography (Bill Lindner, Mike Hehner, Tom Heck, Pete Cozad, Jason Lund)

Additional Photography
Dick Sternberg pp. 18, 27, 69(2), 82(3), 83, 111, 143, 145(3)
Tom Carpenter/NAOG pp. 41, 57(3), 61(3)
Dan Kennedy/NAOG pp. 41, 46
Animals, Animals: ©Robert Maier p. 53; ©LSF, OSF p. 82(3); ©Joe McDonald p. 82; ©Carroll W. Perkins p. 82; ©Bill Beatty p. 83; ©OSF p. 83; ©James H. Robinson p. 83; ©Stephen Dalton p. 83; ©Zig Leszczynski p. 101; ©Ralph Reinhold p.101; ©Leonard Lee Rue III p. 101; ©Allen Blake Sheldon p. 111; ©Fred G. Whitehead p. 112; ©Breck P. Kent/Animals, Animals pp. 112, 113 both; ©Bertram G. Murray Jr. p. 112
Keith Sutton pp. 126, 128
Brook Martin pp. 129(2), 131
John Beath pp. 129, 130(2), 134(3)
Walt Jennings p. 134

Illustration
David Schelitzche pp. 12, 13, 14, 15, 16, 17, 42, 107 both, 130, 131, 139, 149, 151 both
Joe Tomelleri pp. 28 all, 29 all, 30 all, 31 all, 32 all, 33 all
David Rottinghaus pp. 81 all, 119 all

9 8 7 6 5 4 3 2 1

ISBN 1-58159-065-2

North American Fishing Club
12301 Whitewater Drive
Minnetonka, MN 55343

CONTENTS

INTRODUCTION

There is a room in the deepest, darkest corner of my basement that I call my Tackle Room. There is a work bench in there: A double-decker job that runs the length of the room. I haven't seen the top in years because every inch is covered with tackle boxes, utility boxes filled with tackle, and unopened cases of new lures.

So what's my point, besides inviting a break-in? That I love artificial lures. I pick up all the latest baits, and if they work, buy them by the dozen so I have them in every size and color.

But when fishing is tough—and that's often—I will shelve my artificials ... and reach for live bait!

Worms. Minnows. Leeches. Adult insects and larva. Frogs. I have used them all, and others. Successfully. Live bait catches fish, even when artificial lures don't. It's that simple.

It is estimated that 75 percent of all fish caught are fooled by live bait. I'm inclined to agree. And that's why I find a book like this so important. I crave information that will help me find, catch and care for the best live baits available. And while I would like to think I know every rigging method, it is true that I've learned many good ones from this book.

I love fishing artificials. But I love catching fish even more. That's why I love fishing live bait, too.

And you will love this book.

Steve Pennaz

Executive Director
North American Fishing Club

BASIC RIGGING METHODS

Gamefish will turn up their noses at even the freshest, liveliest bait if it isn't rigged properly.

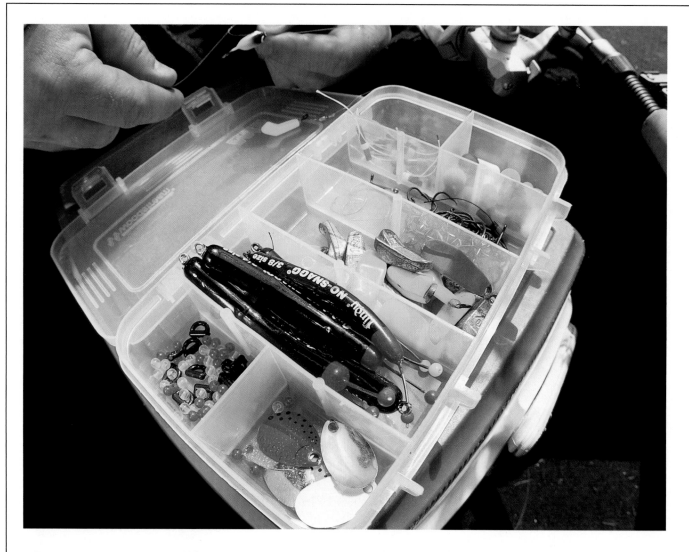

BASIC RIGGING METHODS

According to some estimates, natural bait accounts for three-fourths of all gamefish caught in fresh water. And when the going gets tough, even the staunchest lure chuckers dig into their bait boxes.

While natural bait has a look, smell and action that can't be duplicated by artificials, even the most enticing bait is practically worthless if it isn't rigged properly. It may tear off the hook when you cast, it won't have the right action and, even if a fish grabs it, you probably won't get a good hookset.

Luckily, you don't have to learn a separate rigging method for every different kind of bait. The rigging techniques shown on the following pages (with minor modifications) can be used for a wide variety of baits, for many different fish species and over a broad range of conditions. For example, you can use a slip-bobber rig to catch everything from farm-pond bluegills on waxworms to big-river flatheads on foot-long suckers. All you have to do is change the size and style of float, hook and sinker.

We'll show you all the most popular rigs for presenting natural bait. But before discussing these rigs, you need to understand the components that go into those rigs. Only then will you be able to modify the basic rigs to suit your style of fishing.

Yet the basic rigging methods shown here are not suitable for all types of baits in all situations. You'll have to learn how to make many specialty rigs as well. You'll find these rigs in the chapters dealing with each specific type of bait.

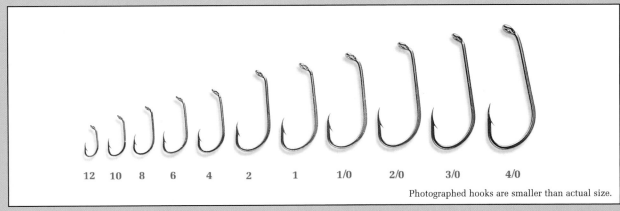

12 10 8 6 4 2 1 1/0 2/0 3/0 4/0

Photographed hooks are smaller than actual size.

Size. *Hook size is designated by a number that reflects the size of the hook's gap, which is the distance between the point and the inside of the shank. For smaller hooks, the number increases as the hooks decrease in size. Larger hooks are measured with a number and an "aught" designation (1/0, 2/0, etc.); the numbers increase as the hooks increase in size.*

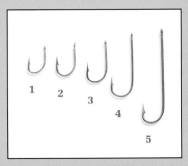

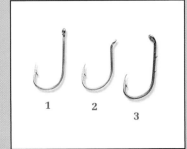

Selecting Hook Size

Fish Type	Hook Size
Largemouth Bass	2–2/0
Smallmouth Bass	6–1
Panfish	12–4
Pike/Muskie	2–8/0
Walleye/Sauger	8–2
Catfish/Sturgeon	1–6/0
Stream Trout	12–2
Lake Trout	2–2/0
Pacific Salmon	4–1/0

Shank Length. *Shank length is designated as (1) extra-short, (2) short, (3) standard, (4) long and (5) extra-long. The length you need depends mainly on the size and shape of your bait. An extra-short shank would be ideal for a salmon egg; a long-shank would be better for a grasshopper or gob of worms.*

Type of Eye. *Most bait fishermen prefer a (1) straight-eye hook, but hooks with a (2) turned-up eye are better for snelling. Some anglers swear by hooks with a (3) turned-down eye which they say improves hooking by directing the hook point into the fish.*

Hook Style. *(1) Round bend, for general-purpose use; (2) Aberdeen, with a thin shank for hooking delicate baits; (3) baitholder, with barbs to prevent bait from sliding down hook shank; (4) claw, with a turned-in point for better hooking; (5) keel, which rotates on the hookset for better penetration; (6) double-needle, for threading on dead baitfish; (7) wide-bend, with a point that is directed toward the eye for stronger hooksets; (8) weedless, for fishing in weedy or brushy cover; (9) sneck, to keep more of the hook point exposed when using large baitfish; (10) Swedish hook, mainly for rigging dead baitfish in ice fishing.*

Selecting Sinkers

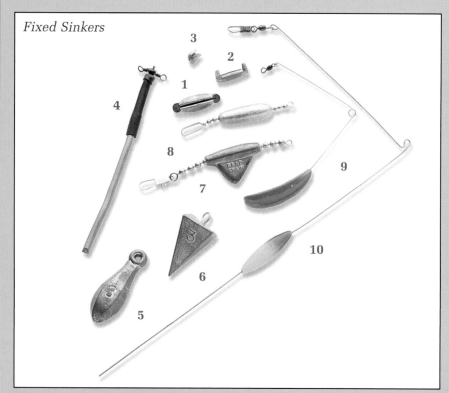

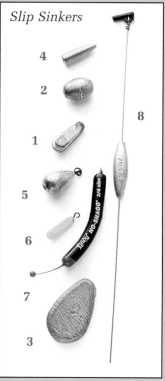

Fixed Sinkers

Slip Sinkers

Fixed Sinkers. *(1) Rubbercor, which twists onto your line; (2) dog-ear and (3) split-shot, which pinch onto your line; (4) surgical tubing with lead insert that can pull out in snaggy cover; (5) bell sinker and (6) pyramid sinker, for dropper rigs; (7) bead chain with keel and (8) bead chain, to minimize line twist; (9) baitwalker and (10) bottom-bouncer, for rocky bottoms.*
Slip Sinkers. *(1) Walking sinker and (2) egg sinker, for general-purpose use; (3) disk sinker, which resists drifting or rolling in current; (4) bullet sinker, for weedy cover; (5 & 6) clip-on sinkers, which enable you to change weights easily; (7) No-Snagg sinker and (8) Slip-Bouncer, for snaggy bottoms.*

Selecting Stops

Selecting Floaters

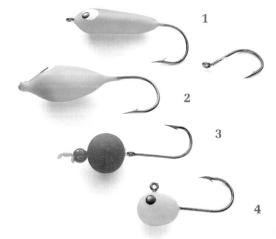

Stops. *(1) slip-knot and bead, (2) split shot, (3) barrel swivel, (4) rubber stop.*

Floaters. *(1) Soft-body floating jig with stinger hook to catch short biters; (2) soft-body floating jig, which has a lifelike feel; (3) Styrofoam ball, which is held in front of the hook by a stop; (4) hardbodied floating jig.*

Selecting Floats

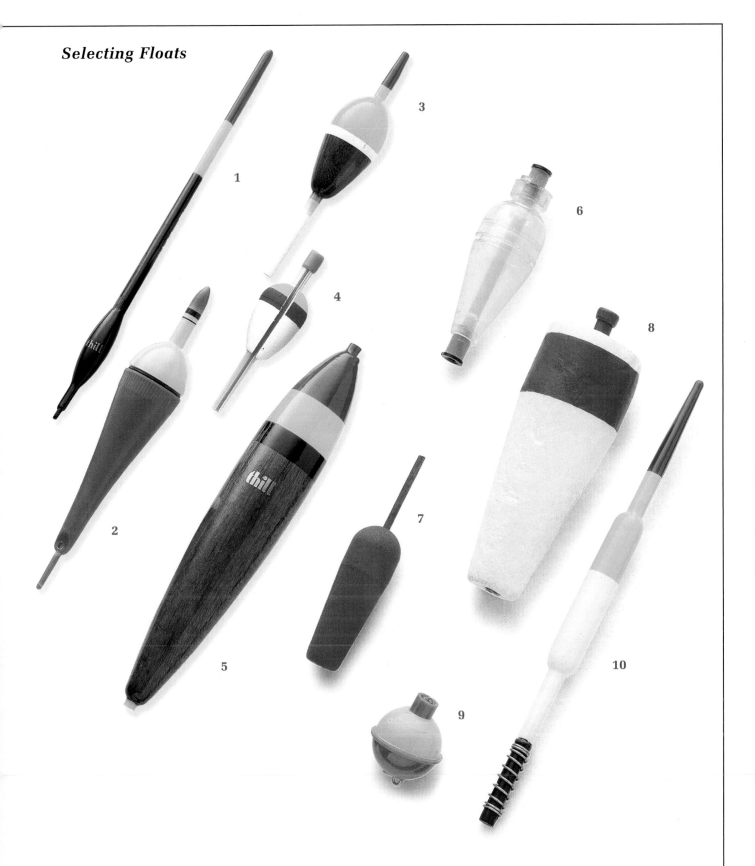

Slip-Bobbers. *(1) European-style, for extra delicacy; (2) lighted slip-bobber, for night fishing; (3) tube-style slip-bobber, which can be adjusted by moving a stop on the line; (4) removable slip-bobber, with a slot that enables you to quickly remove it from your line; (5) cigar float, a slip-bobber for large gamefish.*
Fixed Bobbers. *(6) Casting bubble, which can hold water for extra casting distance; (7) peg-on; (8) weighted casting float, with an internal lead weight; (9) clip-on; (10) spring-lock.*

SLIP-SINKER RIGS

The idea behind a slip-sinker rig is that a fish can pick up your bait and swim away without feeling much resistance. The fish detects nothing out of the ordinary so it is not as likely to drop the bait as it would be if it were towing a heavy sinker.

Another advantage to a slip-sinker rig: Because the sinker is not affixed to the line, you can change weights very easily. This explains why many anglers use slip-sinkers even when fishing with a bobber or using other rigs in which the sinker does not slip.

The basic slip-sinker rig and variations on it are shown below. Functions of the various components are explained on p. 10.

When you detect a bite, release the line. As the sinker rests on the bottom, the fish can swim off without feeling much resistance.

Slip-Sinker Rig Variations

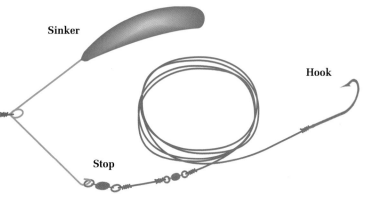

Sinker

Hook

Stop

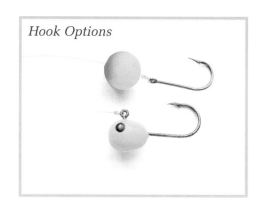

Hook Options

Sinker Options

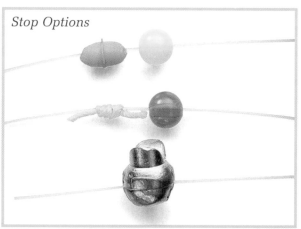

Stop Options

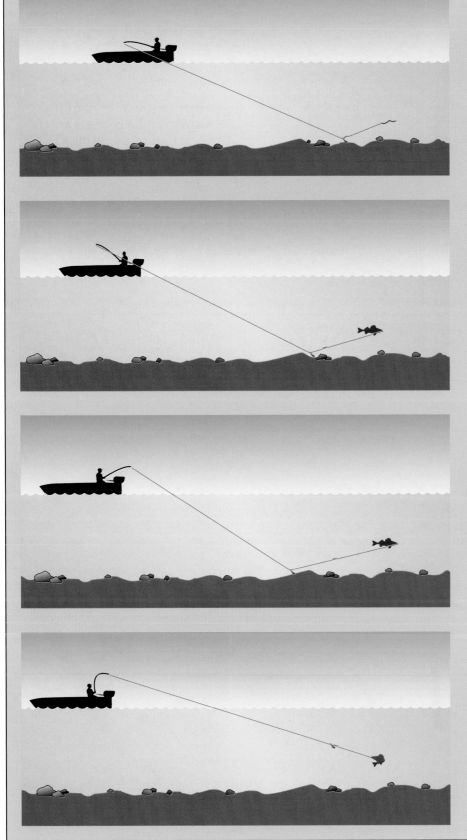

1 Feed line until you feel your sinker hit bottom, then open your bail and hold the line with your finger as you start to troll or drift slowly. You may have to feed a little more line as the boat starts moving, in order to maintain contact with the bottom.

2 When you feel a bite, release the line from your finger so the fish can run without feeling resistance. Before releasing the line, however, you may want to "test" the bite by holding onto the line for a second or two to feel some life. This way, you know you haven't hooked a weed or stick.

3 When you're sure the resistance you feel is a fish, feed line until the fish stops running. Be sure your spool is nearly full and there are no nicks on the rim; otherwise, the line may hang up while the fish is running, causing it to drop the bait.

4 When the fish stops running, rapidly wind up slack until you feel the fish's weight, then set the hook with a sharp upward snap of the wrists. Often, the fish does not swim off in a straight line and in some cases may actually double back on you. If you don't wind up the slack, you probably won't get a firm hookset.

FIXED-SINKER RIGS

With a sinker that is tied in or pinched or twisted onto your line, the rig is not intended to slip when a fish swims off with your bait. This type of rig is most commonly used for large fish that don't mind feeling a little resistance, or fish that bite so aggressively that there is no need to wait for them to swim off before setting the hook. Split-shot rigs are weighted so lightly that fish usually don't notice the slight resistance.

Fixed-sinker rigs offer one big advantage over slip-sinker rigs. Because they don't require a stop, fixed-sinker rigs are easier to tie, and some don't require any tying at all (other than adding a hook). You simply pinch or twist a sinker onto your line and start fishing.

Towing a little extra weight doesn't bother a large and aggressive biter, such as a catfish.

Fixed-Sinker Rig Variations

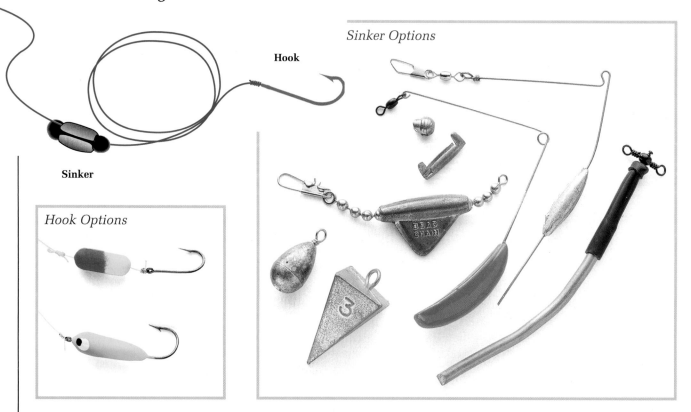

Hook

Sinker

Sinker Options

Hook Options

Fixed-Bobber Rig Variations

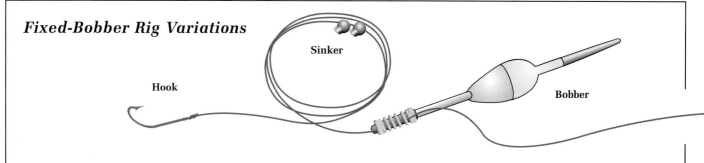

Hook

Sinker

Bobber

Hook Options

Bobber Options

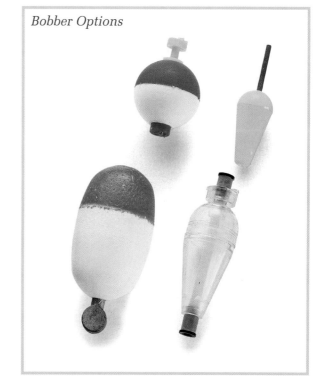

Sinker Options

FIXED-BOBBER RIGS

There's nothing complicated about fishing with a fixed-bobber rig. Just attach a float to your line and balance it with a sinker or enough split shot so it barely floats. This way, a fish can pull it under without feeling much resistance.

Anglers using this technique often make the mistake of using a float that is way too big. Not only does this make it harder to detect bites, it increases the likelihood that a fish will drop the bait.

Because of its simplicity, a fixed-bobber rig is not as likely to tangle as a slip-bobber

A fixed-bobber rig is ideal for fishing pockets in shallow weeds.

rig. And you can cast it a long distance without having to worry about the line catching

on the bobber stop and tearing off your bait.

SLIP-BOBBER RIGS

With a bobber affixed to your line, you're limited to fishing only about 6 feet deep, because you can't cast with more than that much line dangling from the end of your rod. But with a slip-bobber rig, there is no limit on how deep you can fish. You can reel your bait to within a short distance of the rod tip for easy casting, then the line will slip through the float until it reaches a depth determined by where you position the bobber-stop.

Slip-bobber rigs can be used for everything from quarter-pound sunfish to 100-pound catfish. The size of the float you use depends not only on the size of the fish, but on the size of the bait it must support.

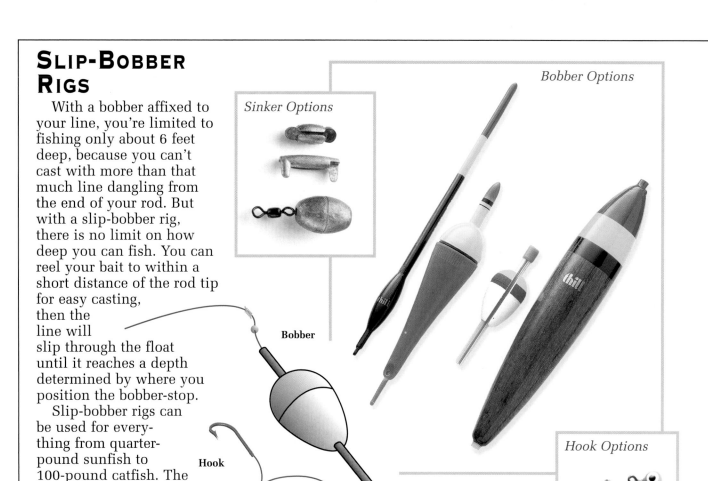

Sinker Options

Bobber Options

Bobber

Hook

Sinker

Hook Options

Slip-Bobber Rig Variations

Lighted bobbers and European-style floats are threaded on through a hole in the bottom. In most cases, the hole is fairly large, so you must use a bead ahead of the bobber stop to prevent it from slipping through the hole.

If you do not have a slip-bobber, substitute a clip-on or peg-on float rigged with a bead and bobber stop. To rig a clip-on, push in the button and turn the wire clip so it rests on the surface of the float as shown.

How a Slip-Bobber Rig Works

1 Reel up enough line so your bait is only 12 to 18 inches from the rod tip. Then, using a sidearm motion, lob the rig gently so the bait does not tear off. Lob-casting also prevents losing your bait should the bobber stop hang up on your spool or in your line guides.

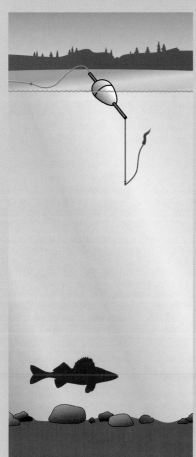

2 Feed line as the bait sinks. The bobber stop will move toward the bobber, which is resting on its side.

3 Continue feeding line as the stop approaches the bobber. If you stop feeding line too soon, the rig will pull back toward you.

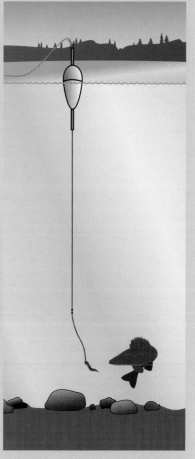

4 When the stop reaches the bobber, the weight will stand it upright and the bait will be at the desired depth.

LURE/BAIT COMBOS

Many kinds of artificial lures are much more effective when tipped with natural bait. The bait not only adds realism, it leaves a scent trail that fish can follow to the lure. But tipping does not work for all lures, because the extra weight of the bait can interfere with the lure's action.

But not all types of bait lend themselves to tipping. Delicate insect baits, for example, are difficult to keep on the hook when casting; and nibbling fish can easily pick them off the hook. And some wiggly baits, such as

Tipping an artificial lure with a leech may not be a good idea.

leeches, tend to wrap themselves around hooks (especially trebles) so the bait doesn't trail properly.

Lures Commonly Tipped with Bait

Leadhead Jig. Tip leadheads with baitfish, worms, leeches, grubs, frogs, salamanders, crayfish, shrimp and cut bait.

Floating Jig. Floaters are commonly tipped with baitfish, worms or leeches. Floaters do not have the buoyancy necessary to lift heavy baits like crayfish or salamanders.

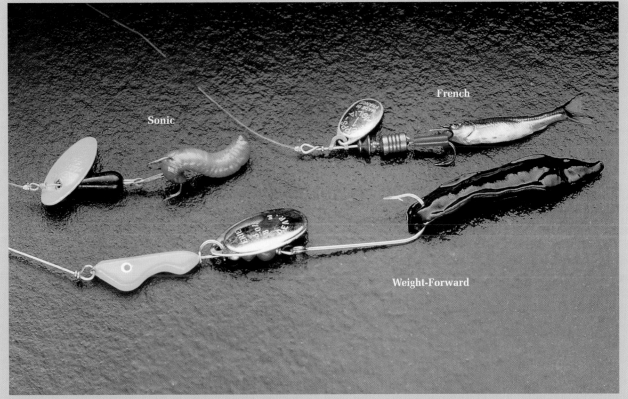

Sonic

French

Weight-Forward

In-Line Spinner. French-style and sonic spinners can be tipped with baitfish or worms. Because of their single hook, weight-forward spinners can also be tipped with leeches.

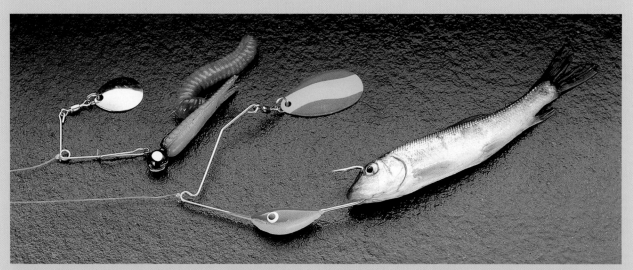

Spinnerbait. *Spin-rigs (left) and jigs with clip-on spinnerbait arms (right) are usually tipped with baitfish, worms or leeches.*

Spinner Rig. *Single-hook spinner rigs (top) are commonly tipped with baitfish, worms or leeches. Multiple-hook rigs (bottom) are designed for nightcrawlers.*

Spin-n-Glo. *Most often, these floating spinner rigs are tipped with fresh spawn, but they can also be tipped with baitfish or nightcrawlers.*

Spoon. *Large spoons have enough "kick" to retain their action when tipped with minnows or strips of cut bait.*

Trolling Plug. *You can tip wide-wobbling plugs, such as a Flatfish, with one or more nightcrawlers.*

Tear Drop. *Tip these tiny lures with grubs, scuds, grass shrimp, small baitfish, or pieces of worms or leeches.*

Jigging Spoon. *Prone to tangling, these lures are often tipped with baitfish, baitfish heads or baitfish eyes.*

BAITFISH

*T*he flash and vibration from a struggling baitfish is a magnet to practically every kind of gamefish.

BAITFISH BASICS

Many kinds of gamefish feed almost exclusively on smaller fish. And as they grow larger, their liking for small fish grows even stronger. So it should come as no surprise that baitfish are the favorite bait of millions of freshwater and saltwater anglers.

The term "baitfish" refers to any small fish that serve as forage for larger fish. Coincidentally, many of the most common baitfish are also popular fishing baits.

To eliminate any confusion as to what the term baitfish means, why not just call any small fish used for bait a "minnow"? That is, in fact, what many anglers do, but the term minnow technically refers only to members of the minnow family, *Cyprinidae*. While many of the most popular baitfish (like chubs and shiners) are minnows, many are not.

How a baitfish is classified, of course, means absolutely nothing to a fish that is about to eat it. What does matter is how the bait looks, smells and swims. Here are the most important bait-selection criteria:

• **Liveliness.** The predatory nature of many gamefish demands that a baitfish look alive. If it's hanging lifelessly on your hook, the fish may swim up to look at it or may even take a nip at it, but probably won't strike aggressively. A baitfish struggling to escape, however, usually

Hardiness of Common Baitfish

Very Hardy	Hardy	Delicate	Very Delicate
Fathead Minnow	Dace (all species)	Common Shiner	Emerald Shiner
Rosy Red	Creek Chub	Golden Shiner	Spottail Shiner
Eel	Redtail Chub	Red Shiner	Cisco
Madtom	Stoneroller	Yellow Perch	Shad
	White Sucker	Killifish	Smelt
	Goldfish		
	Sculpin		
	Bluntnose Minnow		
	Bluegill		

Note: Check your state and local regulations regarding the use of panfish such as bluegill or yellow perch, or exotics such as goldfish, as bait.

draws a vicious strike.

Some types of bait, like emerald shiners, look good at the bait shop; but by the time you get them to the lake, half of them are dead. Others, like fathead minnows, are extremely hardy and will stay alive even if you abuse them. The hardiness of various baitfish species is shown in the chart above.

• **Size.** Predator fish generally prefer a bait of approximately the same size as their natural prey. In fact, size is often the most important consideration.

For example, in early summer when striped bass are feeding on young-of-the-year shad from 2 to 3 inches long, they're not likely to take a 6-inch baitfish. By fall, however, when the year's crop of shad have reached 6 or 7 inches in length, 6-inch baitfish are ideal.

Although shape is not as important as size, it can be a factor as well. When the fish are feeding on deep-bodied forage, deep-bodied baitfish generally work better than long, thin ones.

• **Color/Flash.** As a rule, a bright-colored, flashy baitfish works better than a dark, drab one. In clear water, predators spot the flash from a swimming baitfish from as much as 20 feet away, while they may not even notice a dull-colored baitfish.

But there are exceptions. There will be times when dark-colored baitfish that emit a strong odor will out-produce even the flashiest shiners.

BUYING BAITFISH

It's certainly a lot more convenient to buy baitfish than to collect your own and, in most cases, store-bought baitfish will do the job.

The main drawback to buying your bait is that only a small fraction of the baitfish species shown on the following pages are likely to be available at bait shops in your area. So if you need some other kind of baitfish to appeal to fussy biters, you'll have to learn how to catch your own (pp. 34-39).

Here are some important baitfish-buying tips:
• Be sure you're getting the kind of baitfish you want because bait shops do not adhere to any type of standard nomenclature. For example, fathead minnows may be called "tuffies"; ciscoes, "herring"; madtoms, "willow cats"; etc.
• Make sure the baitfish you buy are healthy (opposite page). If they're sick when you buy them, they'll probably be dead by the time you get them to the water.
• Don't overcrowd your bait bucket. If you buy too many baitfish for the size of your bucket, they will use up the oxygen before you get to your destination. If you need a lot of bait, ask for an oxygen pack or use an aerated bucket (p. 41).
• Be careful about temperature changes. Bait dealers keep their baitfish in very cold water (less than 55°F). If you allow the water to warm rapidly on the way to your destination, you could lose most of your bait. To prevent this problem, some anglers add ice to their bait. But over-icing can be just as detrimental as overwarming. As a rule, you should try to keep the water temperature within a few degrees of that at the bait shop.

Baitfish that form tight clumps near the bottom of the bait tank are healthier than those swimming about in loose formations or near the surface.

Don't buy your bait from a tank with any dark or otherwise discolored baitfish. They may be carrying a disease that has already been transmitted to other baitfish in the tank, weakening them.

Don't buy baitfish with red snouts, missing scales, damaged fins or noticeable patches of white, cottony fungus on the body. These signs of overhandling mean that the bait has been in the tank too long and is not in top condition.

The males of some baitfish, such as fathead minnows (shown) and most chubs, turn dark and develop breeding tubercles on their heads at spawning time. As a rule, the dark-colored males (top) are less effective than the lighter-colored females (bottom).

Popular Kinds of Baitfish

Fathead Minnow (also called tuffie, mudminnow). *Most common in small lakes, ponds and sluggish creeks, fatheads are found throughout most of North America. The first ray of the dorsal fin is very short and the lateral band, unlike that of the bluntnose minnow, does not reach the eye.*

Rosy Red. *The rosy red is a commercially-reared variety of fathead minnow that has been bred to have an orangish or pinkish color.*

Bluntnose Minnow. *The bluntnose prefers larger waters than its close relative, the fathead, but it is found in a wide variety of lakes, ponds and rivers throughout the eastern United States. Like the fathead, it has a short first ray on the dorsal fin, but the lateral band extends to the eye.*

Creek Chub. *As its name suggests, the creek chub resides in creeks and smaller rivers, mainly in the eastern U.S. One of the most common stream minnows, it can be easily distinguished from the hornyhead chub by the black spots at the front of the dorsal fin and base of the tail.*

Hornyhead Chub (also called redtail). *Most common in medium-sized, clear-water streams in the northeastern U.S., the hornyhead chub gets its name from the prominent tubercles on the head of the breeding male. The hornyhead chub resembles the creek chub, but the fins and tail are more reddish.*

Blacknose Dace. *The blacknose dace gets its name from the black lateral band which extends all the way to the nose. The sides are brownish with scattered black scales. Found mainly in the eastern half of the U.S., the blacknose dace inhabits small, fast-moving streams.*

Redbelly Dace (also called rainbow). *Together, the range of the northern and southern redbelly dace covers an area west of the Rockies, from Hudson Bay to Oklahoma. Found mainly in boggy lakes and small- to medium-sized streams, redbellies have a distinct dark lateral band, a second, less-distinct band just above it and a reddish to yellowish belly.*

Golden Shiner. *This deep-bodied baitfish, which is not really a shiner at all, often grows to a foot in length. The sides have a golden hue and the belly has a sharp keel. Although there are scattered pockets of golden shiners in the West, they're found mainly in weedy lakes and ponds in the eastern U.S. and southeastern Canada.*

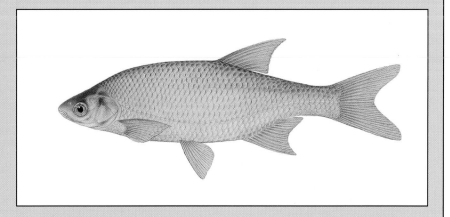

Popular Kinds of Baitfish (Continued)

Emerald Shiner. *It's easy to see where the emerald shiner gets it name—it has an iridescent blue-green back and silvery sides. Found throughout central Canada and the eastern U.S., the emerald shiner inhabits large lakes, reservoirs and rivers.*

Spottail Shiner. *Found in big rivers and big lakes throughout most of Canada and the northeastern U.S., the spottail shiner gets its name from the prominent black spot at the base of the tail. The back is pale olive and the sides are silvery.*

Common Shiner. *This shiner has a deeper body and larger scales than most other shiners. Mainly a stream dweller, the common shiner also inhabits some clearwater lakes. It ranges from southern Saskatchewan to Colorado and then eastward to the Atlantic coast.*

Red Shiner. *Named for the reddish-tinged head, sides and fins of the breeding male, the red shiner has a very deep body—even deeper than that of the common shiner. The red shiner inhabits small streams throughout much of the central and southern U.S. and into northeastern Mexico.*

Goldfish. *This Asian native, a close relative of the carp, has been introduced throughout most of the U.S., mainly by people discarding unwanted aquarium fish. The goldfish thrives in shallow, weedy lakes, reservoirs and streams. It has a deep body that varies in color from green to gold to orange, often with black mottling.*

White Sucker. *Found throughout the northern two-thirds of the U.S. and most of Canada, the white sucker is one of our most common baitfish. Some anglers use suckers weighing more than a pound to catch large catfish, pike and muskies. Suckers have an underslung mouth with large, fleshy lips and drab olive sides with scales that get larger toward the tail.*

Madtom (also called willow cat). *This small, brownish catfish has one continuous fin extending from the middle of the back to the anal fin. The pectoral fins are coated with venom and can inflict a painful sting. Madtoms are most common in medium- to large-sized rivers in the eastern U.S. but are also found in parts of the Northwest.*

Sculpin (also called bullhead, muddler). *Easily identified by its broad head and large pectoral fins, the sculpin is primarily a resident of small streams, but it is also found in large lakes. Sculpins prefer cold water and are most common in the northern half of the U.S., up into Canada and Alaska.*

Shad. *The gizzard shad is hardier than its close relative, the threadfin shad, so it is more commonly used as bait. Gizzard shad inhabit rivers and reservoirs throughout most of the eastern U.S. They have a deep, silvery body, a long ray at the rear of the dorsal fin and a dark spot behind the head.*

Skipjack Herring. *Found primarily in the Mississippi River drainage system, the skipjack herring is easily identified by its protruding lower jaw. It has a bluish to greenish back, silvery sides and a whitish belly. Its extremely oily flesh makes it a favorite of catfish anglers.*

Cisco (also called herring, tullibee). *A resident of large, deep lakes of the northern U.S. and Canada, the cisco makes ideal food for gamefish because of its long, sleek shape. Ciscoes have a greenish back, silvery sides and a small adipose fin behind the dorsal fin.*

Smelt. *This marine species entered the Great Lakes through the St. Lawrence Seaway and has spread to many deep, cold inland lakes in the northern U.S. and Canada. Smelt resemble ciscoes, but their snout is more pointed and they have large teeth.*

Killifish. Many species of killifish live in fresh and brackish waters from southeastern Canada into South America. They are easily identified by their turned-up mouth and dorsal fin positioned far back on the body.

Bluegill. Found throughout most of the U.S., this sunfish inhabits practically all types of warmwater lakes, reservoirs and streams, particularly those with abundant weed growth. The bluegill gets its name from its powder-blue gill cover. It has a black ear lobe and a dark spot at the base of the dorsal fin.

Yellow Perch. Native to most of the northern U.S. and Canada, yellow perch have been widely stocked throughout the South. They thrive in a variety of warmwater and coolwater lakes and streams with sparse to moderate vegetation. Yellow perch have a yellowish coloration with 6 to 8 dark vertical bars on the sides.

American Eel. Eels spawn at sea, but the females spend most of their life in fresh water. They enter rivers along most of the Atlantic and Gulf coasts of North America and often migrate great distances to reach the upstream sections of these waters. Eels are easily identified by the long fin bordering the rear two-thirds of their snakelike body.

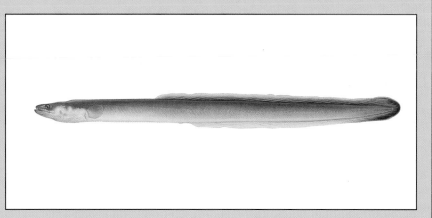

CATCHING BAITFISH

Some of the most effective baitfish are not available at your local bait shop—you have to catch them yourself. That means you'll have to familiarize yourself with the following baitfish-collection methods:

• **Netting.** There are many ways to net your own baitfish. But not all netting methods work in all situations. For example, you could not pull a seine over a bottom strewn with logs, boulders or other obstacles. But you may be able to throw a cast net to catch baitfish in pockets between the obstructions.

The most important netting methods are demonstrated on the upcoming pages.

• **Trapping.** Trapping baitfish is surprisingly easy and, under the right circumstances, extremely effective. Simply set a baited minnow trap in the shallows of a lake, stream or pond and pick it up several hours later or leave it out overnight.

Trapping can be done in most any shallow waters and, unlike some types of netting, does minimal damage to the fish. Common trapping techniques are shown on p. 38.

• **Hook & Line Fishing.** Catching baitfish on hook and line can be almost as much fun as using the bait to catch gamefish! Most baitfish anglers use an ultra-light spinning outfit or a cane pole with a single baited hook, but some use multiple hook set-ups, flies or tiny ice-fishing lures.

Seining

When baitfish are scattered over a large, clean-bottomed flat or pool, seining is likely to be the best collection method. One good seine haul will often catch more baitfish than you could possibly use.

A minnow seine is a long net with mesh no larger than ¼ inch. It has floats along the top, a lead line or lead weights along the bottom and poles or *brails* on the ends. The best seines are made of nylon or other synthetic material that will not rot, even if you put them away wet.

For best results, use a seine at least 25 feet long and 4 feet deep. Baitfish can easily escape a smaller seine. To seine a small area, just roll up

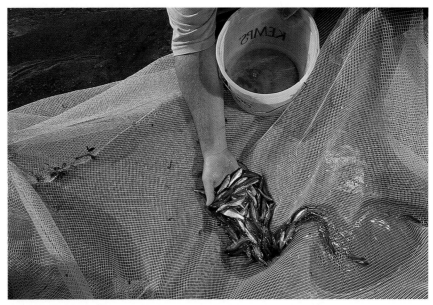

Sort through your catch immediately after beaching the seine. Release any fish of the wrong species or size.

excess netting on the brails.

The photo sequence below demonstrates the basic seining technique.

How to Seine Baitfish

1 Pull the seine along a clean shoreline with the outside seiner walking ahead of the seiner near shore. Tilt the brails as shown and keep them right on the bottom.

2 Near the end of the haul, the inside seiner stops, forming a pivot point for the outside seiner who closes the net by walking toward shore.

3 Once the brails are on shore, each seiner kneels down and slowly pulls the net in by hand so the lead line stays on the bottom. If you pull too fast or lift the lead line, most of the bait will escape.

Cast Netting

Throwing a cast net requires some practice, but once you perfect the technique you'll be able to catch a variety of baitfish in many different habitats.

A cast net is a round nylon net with lead weights around the perimeter. A draw string in the middle enables you to gather the mesh and trap the baitfish once the net is sunk.

Be sure to select a quality net. They cast easier, open flatter, sink quicker and last longer than cheaper models.

Cast nets are measured in feet, according to their radius. A 5-foot net, for example, opens to a diameter of 10 feet. A 5- or 6-foot net is adequate for most anglers and is the best size for an inexperienced thrower. Guides or commercial fishermen who need more bait may use a 7- or 8-footer. As a rule, you'll need at least one pound of lead for every foot of net radius.

Unlike seining, cast-netting is a one-man method. You simply walk or boat around a likely area until you spot the baitfish, and then throw the net over them as shown in the photos below.

How to Use a Cast Net (Right-handed Thrower)

1 Loop the handline around your left wrist, hold coils of the line in your left hand and use the same hand to grasp the rear of the net. Hold the lead line with your right hand.

2 Throw the net with your right hand, using your arms and shoulders along with a twisting motion at the waist to spin the net.

3 If thrown properly, the net should open into a full circle, land on top of a baitfish school, and sink quickly to entrap them.

4 Let the net sink for a few seconds, then sharply pull on the handline to close the net. Retrieve the net and open it to remove the baitfish.

Speed is the key to dip netting baitfish. When you spot a tight school, plunge the net into the water, sweep it through the school rapidly and then lift it out of the water before the fish can escape.

Dip Netting

When you find baitfish tightly concentrated in a small area, such as an eddy at the base of a dam, you may be able to catch them with a dip net.

Dip nets also work well in tight spots, such as an eddy behind a boulder in a small stream. Some anglers use strong lights to draw baitfish to docks or piers at night, and then use a dip net to catch them.

Most dip nets have small-mesh nylon netting on a 1- to 2-foot diameter metal hoop and a handle at least 6 feet in length. To ensure that the baitfish you catch cannot jump out, the net should be at least 2 feet deep.

You can buy dip nets with wire mesh, but they are more likely to scrape off scales and slime or otherwise injure the bait.

Umbrella Netting

Many anglers are unfamiliar with umbrella nets, but these simple devices work surprisingly well for catching baitfish from piers, docks and even anchored boats.

An umbrella net, also called a drop net, looks like an umbrella turned upside down. It consists of a nylon net from 3 to 4 feet square with a wire frame to keep it spread. It is lowered into the water with a cord attached to the top of the frame.

You can buy umbrella nets and most of the other nets shown on these pages from commercial-fishing supply houses and some larger bait shops.

Lower an umbrella net to the bottom. If you see baitfish on top of the net, pull it up quickly to catch them. Or, just wait for a few minutes and then make a blind lift. If desired, put some chum in the net area to attract the bait.

Trapping

Commercially made wire-mesh minnow traps are inexpensive and easy to use. Funnels at each end lead the baitfish into the trap. Once inside, the baitfish cannot escape. These traps are available at most bait shops and through many fishing-tackle catalogs.

Minnow traps are normally set in late afternoon or evening and picked up the next day. But in extremely fertile lakes or streams, you may have to pick them up before dark. Otherwise, the baitfish you catch may die from oxygen depletion in the shallows during the night.

Madtoms are an extremely effective bait, but they commonly inhabit dense vegetation so they're difficult to catch. Like other catfish, they have a habit of swimming into cavities in the bank and other enclosed spots. Innovative anglers use this habit to their advantage by setting out strings of pop cans which serve as tiny traps.

Open the trap and bait it with bread, crackers or dog food. Weight it with rocks to prevent it from drifting with the current or blowing into shore from wave action. In streams, point a funnel into the current.

Check the trap by lifting it from the water and turning it upright so the baitfish are all on one end. Then open the trap and pour the baitfish into a minnow bucket.

Make a pop-can trap by tying a nylon cord to the tabs of several cans so they are 1 to 3 feet apart. Sink the cans in a weedy backwater or slack-water zone of a big river known to hold madtoms. When you pick up the cans the next day, you'll catch any madtoms that swim into the cans to find cover.

Hook & Line Fishing

If there is a small creek or pond near your home, you probably have an inexhaustible supply of baitfish that can easily be caught on hook and line. And you'll probably be able to catch them from shore. Of course, you can catch baitfish on larger waters as well, but they may be more difficult to find and you'll probably need a boat to reach them.

In most cases, all you have to do is grab an ultralight spinning outfit spooled with 2-pound-test mono, add a split shot and a size 12 to 18 hook (or multiple-hook rig), and bait up with a tiny piece of worm. Some anglers prefer an extension pole or cane pole to fish pockets in weedy or brushy cover.

Small streams hold a wide variety of baitfish including suckers, chubs, dace and shiners.

At times, you'll see baitfish dimpling the surface as they take small insects. That's the time to break out your fly rod and tie on a tiny dry fly. Or, when the fish aren't dimpling, work the bottom with a small nymph.

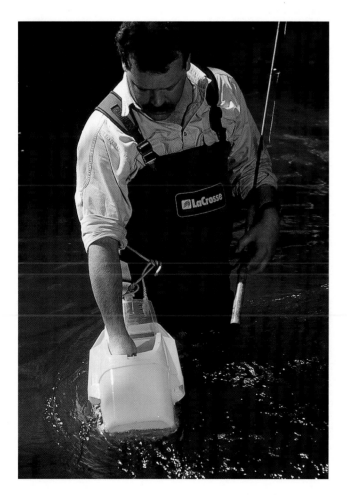

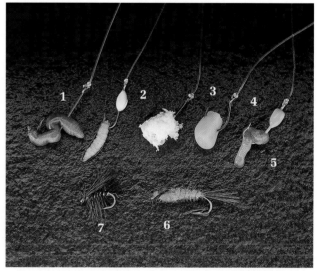

Popular baits and lures for catching baitfish on hook and line include (1) bit of worm, (2) maggot, (3) bread ball, (4) corn kernel, (5) tear drop and bit of worm, (6) nymph and (7) dry fly.

When wading to catch baitfish, tie a floating bait bucket to your belt. This way, you won't have to walk back to shore every time you catch a fish.

KEEPING BAITFISH

Whether you buy your baitfish or catch your own, you must keep them healthy until you're ready to use them. That's not difficult when you're dealing with hardy baitfish species (p. 25), but it's a big problem with delicate species, especially in warm weather.

Baitfish are more difficult to keep alive when the water is warm, for two reasons: Their metabolism is higher, so they require more oxygen, and warm water does not hold as much oxygen as cold water. This explains why bait dealers keep their baitfish in cold water (usually less than 55°F) and why you should too.

To maintain that temperature in warm weather, you'll have to add ice to your bucket. But don't add too much; overchilling the baitfish is just as bad as overwarming them.

It's best to keep baitfish in water from the lake or stream in which you caught them. When you have to change water, use well water or tap water treated with a dechlorinator. Another option is to use tap water that has been allowed to stand overnight and dechlorinate naturally.

There is no firm rule as to how often the water must be changed; it depends on how many baitfish you're keeping and the water temperature. To be safe, it's a good idea to change water every day to prevent a build up of ammonia, which could kill the bait.

While on the water, you can keep your bait alive in a flow-through bucket. But unless the water temperature is cool, that method may not work well for sensitive baitfish like shiners. To keep them alive in warm weather, you'll need an insulated, aerated bucket, adding ice as needed.

Popular minnow buckets include: (1) Styrofoam, which "breathes"; (2) plastic and (3) metal buckets with perforated inserts; (4) flow-through; and (5) aerated bucket, which runs off a boat's 12-volt electrical system.

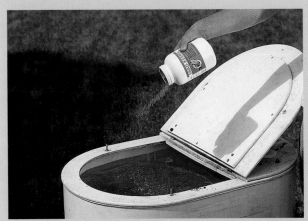

Chemically treat the water to add electrolytes and enhance the bait's slime coat. A variety of chemicals are available, some of which are specific to certain kinds of baitfish.

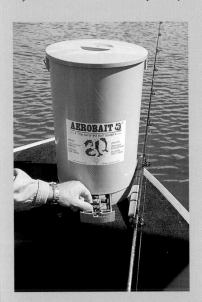

Portable, battery-powered aerators are ideal for keeping large numbers of baitfish alive for a prolonged period. Most require 6- to 12-volt D.C. power sources, but some also operate on 110-volt A.C.

Large, delicate baitfish such as shad will not stay alive in an ordinary minnow bucket, so you'll need an insulated, aerated tank that holds 30 to 50 gallons of water. For long-term storage, some anglers use lakeside tanks that hold 500 to 1,000 gallons.

Add oxygen tablets to the water to provide the short-term source of oxygen needed to transport baitfish to your destination, and to keep them lively while you fish.

To keep baitfish alive on a long trip, ask the bait shop for an oxygen pack, a heavy plastic bag filled with water and pure oxygen. An oxygen pack will keep the bait alive for 2 or 3 days.

FISHING WITH BAITFISH

Anglers use baitfish to catch practically every kind of freshwater gamefish, from 6-inch perch to 10-foot sturgeon. And there are just about as many ways to rig and fish baitfish as there are kinds of gamefish that will take them.

The rigging method depends mainly on the size and shape of the baitfish and whether you're fishing them alive or dead. The most popular rigging methods are listed on the opposite page.

Your hooking method is of utmost importance. A baitfish that is small in comparison to the size of the fish being targeted can be hooked most anywhere—through the lips, roof of the mouth, back or tail. But a comparatively larger baitfish is much harder to swallow, so the hooking options are more limited.

Most gamefish catch baitfish however they can—by the head, sideways or by the tail. But they almost always swallow them head-first. This way, their meal slides down easily and the fins fold back neatly so they don't catch in the fish's throat. This explains why anglers using very large baitfish often hook them in the head or use some sort of harness, with one hook near the front and another farther back.

Tail-hooking large baitfish is risky; unless the fish happens to grab the bait tail-first and you set the hook right away, you probably won't hook up.

A long, thin-bodied baitfish gives you more hooking options than one with a deep body. If you tried to hook a deep-bodied baitfish, like a bluegill, in the lips, you'd probably pull it out of the fish's mouth. With a thin-bodied baitfish, the barb is more likely to catch in the mouth. As a rule deep-bodied baitfish should be hooked

It's easy to see why deep-bodied baitfish shouldn't be lip-hooked.

through the back.

Most anglers use live baitfish, because that's what the majority of gamefish prefer. But baitfish can also be fished dead to catch scent-feeders like catfish and lake trout. Or, they can be used as cut bait.

Popular Baitfish-Rigging Methods

Species of Gamefish	Size/Type of Baitfish	Popular Rigging Methods
Panfish (crappies, sunfish, rock bass, warmouth, yellow perch, white perch, white bass)	1½- to 3-inch fathead minnows, shiners and redbelly dace (rainbows).	• Bobber rig with plain hook, small jig or tear drop • Welding-rod rig (crappie stick) • Jig and minnow or inch-long strip of cut bait • Tandem-hook (tightline) rig • Beetle-Spin and minnow • Jigging spoon and minnow head
Walleye, sauger, smallmouth bass	2½- to 4-inch fathead minnows, bluntnose minnows, shiners, chubs, dace and madtoms.	• Slip-bobber rig with plain hook or small jig • Slip-sinker rig with plain hook or floater • Split-shot rig • Jig and minnow • Spinner rig with slip-sinker or bottom bouncer • Jigging spoon with whole minnow or minnow head • Spin-rig and minnow
Northern pike, muskie	4- to 12-inch suckers, chubs, shiners, goldfish, yellow perch, smelt and ciscoes. For trophy fish, some anglers use baitfish up to 15 inches long.	• Slip-bobber rig with wire leader and plain hook, Swedish hook or quick-strike rig • Slip-sinker rig with wire leader and plain or weedless hook • Off-bottom rig with wire leader • Jig and minnow with wire leader • Strip-on spinner and minnow with wire leader
Largemouth bass	4-8 inch golden shiners, shad, chubs, dace and killifish; eels up to 12 inches long.	• Freelining with weedless hook • Peg-on float with weedless hook • Slip-sinker rig with plain or weedless hook • Slip-bobber rig with plain hook
Catfish	4- to 12-inch suckers, chubs, shiners, shad, skipjack, goldfish, carp and bluegills; mackerel and bonito for cut bait.	• Slip-sinker rig with egg or disk sinker and plain hook • Slip-sinker floating rig • 3-way swivel rig with bell sinker or bottom bouncer • Tandem-hook dropper rig • Slip-bobber rig
Striped bass	6- to 12-inch shad, skipjack, golden shiners, bluegills, chubs and frozen anchovies; eels up to 18 inches long.	• Jig tipped with minnow or "pencil" eel • Casting bobber with jig and minnow • Balloon or slip-bobber rig with plain hook
Trout	3- to 12-inch smelt, ciscoes, shiners, chubs, suckers and sculpins.	• Slip-sinker rig and plain hook with minnow or cut bait • Jig tipped with minnow or cut bait • Heavy spoon tipped with cut bait • Needle-hook rig
Salmon	4- to 8-inch smelt, ciscoes and shiners. Coastal anglers use herring; Great Lakes anglers, alewives.	• Slip-sinker rig with floater • Trolling harness • Mooching rig

Basic Baitfish-Hooking Methods

Through Lips. *Push your hook through the lips of a thin-bodied baitfish from the bottom up. The bait will stay lively, and trail naturally when you're casting or trolling.*

Through Snout. *Also used for thin-bodied baitfish, this hooking method leaves more of the hook point exposed, increasing your chances of the barb penetrating when you set the hook.*

Out Gill and Through Back. *Using a long-shank hook, push the hook point through the mouth, out the gill and through the back. This method holds the baitfish securely but usually kills it.*

Through Nostrils. *Commonly used for shad, this hooking method directs the hook point to the side, rather than the top, of the head. This way, when the bait is lying flat in a fish's mouth, the hook is pointing toward the top or bottom of the fish's mouth.*

Through Tail. *This is the best way to hook baitfish for freelining, but it also works well for slow-trolling or casting; when pulled backward, the baitfish struggles more than it otherwise would.*

Through Back. *This method works well for still-fishing with either deep- or thin-bodied baitfish. Try to position the hook so the baitfish balances horizontally.*

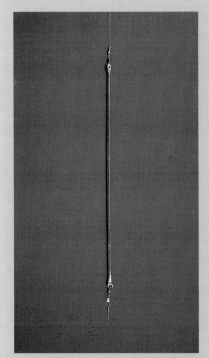

To prevent crappies or other panfish from tangling your line in brushy cover, use a "crappie stick." Flatten the ends of a welding rod and drill holes in each end. Add a split ring and long-shank, light-wire hook to one end and a split ring or snap-swivel to the other (left). The rod makes it much more difficult for a fish (or your minnow) to tangle your line in the brush (right). Should you get snagged, just let the rod drop freely; the downward force of the weight is usually enough to free the hook.

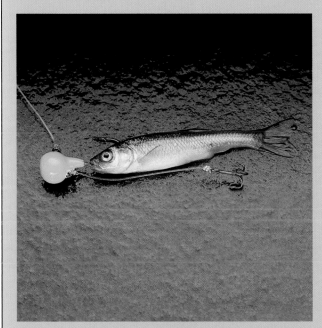

A jig and minnow is a deadly bait for walleyes, bass, pike and panfish, but there will be times when the fish strike short. To solve the problem, use a jig head with an extra eye and attach a treble "stinger hook." Let it trail free rather than hooking it in the minnow's tail.

Use a quick-strike rig to fish large baitfish (live or dead) for pike and muskies. Push one hook into the body near the pectoral fin and the other in front of the dorsal. When a fish strikes, set the hook immediately.

Freeline a large baitfish in heavy vegetation to catch big largemouths. Hook the bait just above the anal fin with a size 2/0 to 4/0 weedless hook and feed line as it swims through the weeds.

A wire leader is a must when using large baitfish to catch pike and muskies. But ordinary wire leaders tend to kink. To solve the problem, substitute a titanium leader which is nearly impossible to kink.

Used mainly for pike, an off-bottom rig keeps a large baitfish close to, but not on, the bottom. A sinker maintains bottom contact while the bait is held above the bottom by a float and wire arm.

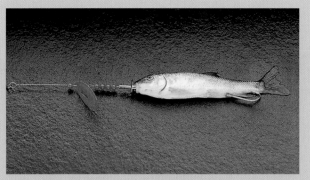

Strip-on Spinner. *Remove the double hook and then push the wire through the mouth of a large bait-fish and out the vent (left). Then replace the double hook by pushing it through the opening in the wire with the points up (right). Strip-ons are most commonly used for pike and muskies but are also effective for big bass, stripers, lake trout and other large predator fish.*

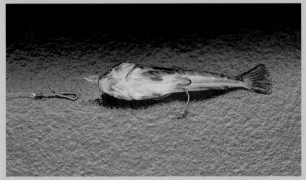

Needle Hook. *Popular for fishing sculpins for trout in western streams, the needle hook can be used for rigging practically any kind of dead baitfish. Push the "needle" through the vent and out the mouth (left). Then attach the clip to the hole in the needle (right). This way the bait can swing freely on the clip.*

Mooching Rig. *Popular for salmonids in coastal waters of the Pacific Northwest, mooching rigs are also used in the Great Lakes and other inland waters. The rig consists of a pair of single hooks, one of which slides on the line so the rig can be adjusted to the length of the bait. Push the rear hook through the tail and the front hook through the head (top). Then adjust the position of the front hook to snug up the line (bottom).*

Swedish Hook. *These unusual hooks are used mainly for fishing smelt, ciscoes or other dead baits for pike. With the hook shank down, push the hook into the vent up to the bend (left). Then rotate the hook so the shank is up and push the point through the back (right). Rigged properly, the bait should ride horizontally in the water.*

Threading On. *Use a bait needle to push your line through the mouth of a baitfish and out the vent (left). Remove the needle then tie on a treble hook; pull on the line to draw the shaft of the hook into the vent (right).*

Throat Latch. *Should you run out of bait, remove the throat latch from a walleye or perch you've already caught by cutting along the dotted line (left). Fish the throat latch on a plain hook or use it to tip a jig (right). The throat latch emits scent, wiggles enticingly and is remarkably durable.*

Plug-Cut Baitfish. "Plug-cutting" means slicing off the head of a baitfish at an angle so the bait rolls slowly when you're drifting or slow-trolling for salmonids. First, angle your cut from top to bottom and from side to side (1). Remove the innards. Then push the rear hook of a mooching rig (2) into the body and out the side above the vent (3). Finally, push the front hook through the back so it pierces the backbone and adjust the position of the hook to take up most, but not all, of the slack.

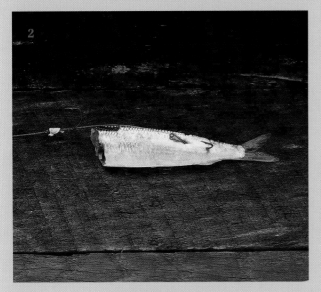

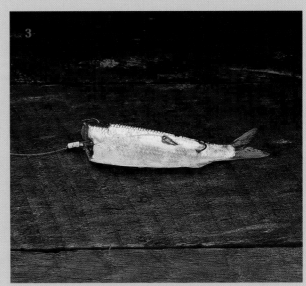

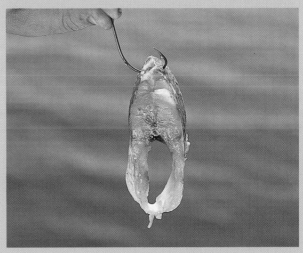

Chunk Bait. Cut a good-sized shad, skipjack herring or other oily baitfish into inch-wide chunks (left) to catch catfish. Push the hook through the back (right), leaving plenty of the hook point exposed.

WORMS

*W*orms are the oldest known fish bait, and they are no less effective today than they were centuries ago.

Live Bait

WORM BASICS

Worms are a near-universal bait for freshwater gamefish. They will catch everything from sunfish to sturgeon, and even toothy predators like pike don't hesitate to gobble up a lively nightcrawler.

Besides their amazing fish appeal, there are many other reasons for the popularity of worms:

• They are one of the easiest baits to find. After a good rain you can probably find enough worms for several fishing trips by picking them up on your lawn or a nearby golf course.

• Worms are easier to keep alive than most other kinds of bait. Most species of worms will live for weeks in a can of black dirt kept in a cool spot.

• Many species of worms are surprisingly easy to raise. Avid worm fishermen often have a "worm box" in their basement or backyard to give them a permanent supply.

Most kinds of worms thrive in fertile, loamy soil. But some can be found in soil consisting mainly of sand or clay. Worms feed by eating their way through the ground, leaving a trail of castings that further enrich the soil.

Worms are *hermaphrodites*, meaning that each individual possesses male and female sex organs, which are found in the dark band, or collar, near the head. An individual cannot fertilize its own eggs but, when two individuals breed (right), both are impregnated and produce a cocoon filled with eggs that is deposited in the soil. In about 2 or 3 weeks, tiny worms emerge from the cocoon to begin life on their own.

Worms have another unique property: They can be broken into pieces without killing them. When you're fishing for small gamefish, just break off a small piece of a worm—it will stay alive and wiggly for quite awhile. If you're after big fish, thread several worms onto the hook to create a writhing gob that fish find hard to resist.

Although worms do not have eyes or ears, they can sense the presence of predators (or humans attempting to catch them) by detecting subtle ground vibrations. Their body is also equipped with light-sensitive cells, explaining why they seldom come out of their burrows during the day and why they rapidly dart back into them when struck by the beam of a flashlight.

Nightcrawlers and some other kinds of worms breed on rainy nights, lying side by side on the ground and joining at the collar to fertilize each other's eggs.

Common Nightcrawler. *One of the most widely distributed worms, the common nightcrawler is sometimes called the "dew worm" because it comes out of its burrow on cool, dewy or rainy nights. These big worms are 6 to 10 inches long, varying in color from brownish to pinkish to purplish, with a darker collar.*

European Nightcrawler. *These worms, available from many commercial growers, resemble common nightcrawlers but have a much slimmer body.*

African Nightcrawler. *Like gray nightcrawlers, African nightcrawlers are grown commercially and are exceptionally lively. But they are more heat-tolerant and can be kept at room temperature. Similar in color to common nightcrawlers, they range from 3 to 5 inches in length.*

Other Common Types of Worms

Grunt Worm. The term "grunt worm" refers to any of several large worms commonly taken by "grunting" or "fiddling" (p. 57). These worms vary in color from pinkish to brownish to grayish, with no distinct collar, and range in length from 5 to 8 inches.

Garden Worm. Perhaps the most common of all fishing worms, the garden worm is commonly called the "angleworm." Garden worms are usually 3 to 4 inches long and vary in color from pinkish to grayish to bluish, with a collar only slightly darker than the rest of the body.

Red Wiggler. A favorite of panfish anglers, these lively, commercially grown worms run only 1½ to 3 inches in length. Dark reddish in color, red wigglers are also called "manure worms" because they thrive in compost piles.

Leaf Worm. Commonly found under leaves and logs, these worms resemble miniature common nightcrawlers. They range in length from 3 to 4 inches.

On a drizzly spring night, look for nightcrawlers on a well-established, short-grass lawn or a golf course that is not treated with chemicals to control worm numbers. Walk softly to minimize vibrations and use a flashlight with colored cellophane (usually red) over the lens to prevent spooking. When you spot a crawler, grab it quickly by the head and, if necessary, pull gently to dislodge it from its burrow.

COLLECTING WORMS

Anglers who collect their own worms know that weather conditions make a big difference in their success. As a rule, it's easiest to find worms in cool, damp weather; most difficult in hot, dry weather.

When it's cool and moist, worms are generally found in the top foot or two of soil. When it's hot and dry, they go deeper—often much deeper. The common nightcrawler may burrow to depths of 15 feet to find the cool, moist conditions it requires. Other types of worms rarely go that deep, but they burrow to depths where they're nearly impossible to reach by digging.

Shown here are some tips for collecting the most popular types of worms.

Draw grunt worms to the surface by driving a board with series of saw kerfs into the ground and then rubbing an ax handle up and down the board to create vibrations in the soil. This technique, called "fiddling" or "grunting," is usually done in pine forests in the southeastern states.

Dig for red wigglers (manure worms) in a compost pile. The worms are usually within 12 to 18 inches of the surface of the pile. Many anglers make their own compost pile from leaves, grass trimmings, coffee grounds and other garbage.

Pick up nightcrawlers and other worms on the road early in the morning after a heavy rain. Use a spatula to pick them up quickly. If you wait until later in the morning, the worms will get eaten by birds or squashed by cars.

Use a pitchfork to unearth garden worms (and sometimes nightcrawlers and leaf worms) in moist soil. If you use a spade, you'll slice many of the worms in half. If the ground is dry, water it thoroughly the day before you dig.

Roll over logs or pick up boards, leaves or other objects to find leaf worms. Confine your search to areas where the soil is moist; if it's too dry, the worms will not be on the surface.

The best commercial worm containers are made from breathable materials such as (1) Styrofoam or (2) fiberboard. These materials not only are good insulators, they are impervious to water yet allow air to penetrate, keeping the worms well-oxygenated. Many anglers make their own (3) wooden worm boxes with a screen cover.

KEEPING WORMS

When conditions are right, you can easily collect enough worms for a month of fishing in only an hour or two. But then you're faced with a more difficult challenge: How to keep them alive long enough to reap the benefits.

If you put your worms in a tin can and set them in a corner of your garage, they may last for a few days. But if it gets hot, you'll end up with a goopy, foul-smelling mess.

The secret to keeping worms alive for long periods of time is putting them in the right kind of medium (in the right container) and controlling the temperature and moisture content.

If you gather your own worms, you can keep them in the same kind of soil from which they were collected. But they'll stay alive longer and be healthier if you keep them in a commercial worm bedding consisting of a mixture of ground-up paper products and black dirt. If you raise red wigglers or other worms purchased from commercial growers, you'll probably want to keep them in the type of commercial bedding recommended by the grower.

Many bedding mixtures contain a supply of food that should last for several weeks. After that, you'll have to add food to sustain your worm crop. Red wigglers also thrive in compost piles that are continually nourished with food scraps.

Many anglers store a large supply of worms in a worm box (opposite) kept in a refrigerator or cool spot in their basement. For a day of fishing, they remove only what's needed, keeping them in a smaller worm box or a cooler filled with worm bedding or sphagnum moss.

1 Fill a Styrofoam or wooden worm box with bedding, then add water to moisten it. Knead the bedding to soak up the water and keep adding water until all of the bedding is just moist enough that you can barely wring water out of it. The bedding will compress as it is moistened, so you must keep adding bedding and water until the box is filled to a depth of about 4 inches.

2 Sprinkle worms you've collected or purchased on top of the bedding. Check in a few hours to be sure all the worms have tunneled into the bedding; discard those that have not. As a rule, 1 square foot of bedding will support 4 or 5 dozen nightcrawlers or 12 to 15 dozen smaller worms.

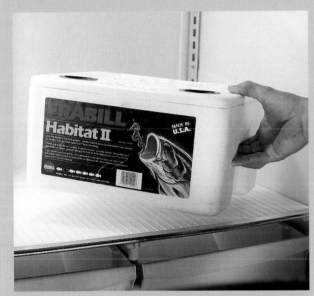

3 Keep your worm box in an old refrigerator or a cool corner of your basement. Although different kinds of worms prefer different temperatures, most do well at temperatures in the 45 to 60°F range. If you keep your worms at temperatures below 40, they probably won't feed. Check the bedding every week or so and remove any dead worms.

4 If you plan on keeping the worms more than a couple months, feed them commercial worm food. Just sprinkle a little food on top of the bedding every few days; this way, you can tell if the worms are eating it. If not, discontinue feeding because the uneaten food will rot and contaminate the bedding.

How to Raise Worms

Commercial worm producers sell red wigglers and other varieties of worms that can be used to seed compost piles and worm pits, providing anglers with a permanent supply of prime fishing bait. In areas where the ground freezes in winter, fishermen keep their worm boxes in their basement. The worms reproduce rapidly and will double in number about every 60 days at temperatures in the mid-50s to mid-70s.

Raise worms in a compost pile made from leaves and grass clippings and enriched with horse or cow manure and vegetable scraps. Sprinkle worms over the pile at a rate of about ½ pound per square foot. Periodically add more vegetable scraps for food.

How to Make & Use a Worm Pit

1 Make a wooden box ranging in size from 3'x2'x1' to 4'x3'x2' (length, width, depth). If you're raising red wigglers, there is no reason to make the pit any more than a foot deep, because the worms are surface feeders. Make a cover to keep out insects and rodents. Drill ¼-inch holes in the bottom for ventilation, then sink the box into a hole you've dug in the ground. Be sure to dig your pit in an area that won't freeze or overheat.

2 Fill the box with commercial bedding or make your own bedding from shredded newspaper moistened to the dampness of a wrung-out sponge. Do not use glossy paper or any paper with colored ink. Add a little rich black dirt to the newspaper.

3 Seed the box with several hundred worms. Feed them fruit and vegetable scraps, pasta, bread, coffee grounds and eggshells (for calcium). The worms will not eat animal products such as meat or cheese.

Tips for Keeping Worms in Good Condition

To prevent getting worm bedding all over your boat, remove your worms from the bedding and put them in pail full of ice. The meltwater cleans the worms and they'll stay alive all day.

When fishing in hot weather, keep your worms in a bedding-filled lunch cooler with an ice pack in the lid. Or put some ice cubes in a small resealable plastic bag (shown) and place it under the bedding.

Periodically inspect your worm box and remove any dead ones. If left in the box too long, the dead worms will foul the bedding and kill the rest of the worms.

To keep your compost pile or worm pit from drying out, cover it with cardboard, wet the cardboard with a hose and then add a layer of straw. When the cardboard dries out, wet it down again.

FISHING WITH WORMS

Other than the rare occasions when heavy rains wash earthworms into lakes and streams, gamefish seldom encounter earthworms in their natural environment. Nevertheless, earthworms will catch practically every kind of gamefish that swims in fresh water. Even large fish eaters like northern pike or striped bass will occasionally take a nightcrawler.

The most likely reason that fish bite on earthworms is that the fish feed on aquatic insect larvae that resemble worms. Walleyes, for example, commonly eat midge larvae or "bloodworms" that look like miniature red wigglers.

One important consideration in choosing worms is size. A single nightcrawler is the best choice for most large gamefish, but for giant catfish and sturgeon, some anglers gob on as many as 6 crawlers. Panfish and other small gamefish will take a whole crawler, but they'll probably just nip off the end. A 2- or 3-inch garden worm or red wiggler is a better choice.

Equally important is freshness of your bait. A lively, squirming worm will draw more strikes than a squishy, lifeless one. Even if a fish takes a dead worm, there's a good chance it will spit it out before you can set the hook.

Popular Worm-Rigging Methods

Species of Gamefish	Size/Type of Worm	Popular Rigging Methods
Panfish (sunfish, rock bass, warmouth, yellow perch, white perch)	Garden worms, red wigglers, leaf worms and other worms from $1^1/2$ to 4 inches in length; pieces of nightcrawler.	• Small float (fixed, slip or casting bubble), split shot and plain hook • In-line spinners and small spinnerbaits tipped with pieces of worm • Plain hook and split shot fished on a cane pole or extension pole • Plain hook on a "hanger" rig (yellow perch) • Small jig tipped with piece of worm
Walleye and sauger	4- to 8-inch nightcrawlers (plain or inflated).	• Slip-sinker rig with plain short-shank hook or floater • Slip-bobber rig with plain short-shank hook or $1/16$-ounce jig head • Split-shot rig and plain hook • Weight-forward spinner or spin-rig tipped with nightcrawler • Bottom-walker rig with spinner and double- or triple-hook crawler harness • Trolling plug tipped with crawlers
Smallmouth and largemouth bass	4- to 8-inch nightcrawlers (plain or inflated).	• Slip-sinker rig with plain short-shank hook or floater • Split-shot rig and plain hook • Slip-bobber rig with plain short-shank hook or $1/16$-ounce jig head • Spin-rig tipped with nightcrawler
Catfish	4- to 8-inch nightcrawlers.	• Fixed or slip-sinker rig with 2 to 6 worms gobbed onto plain or treble hook • Slip-bobber rig with 2 or 3 worms gobbed onto plain hook • Plain hook with gob of worms on jug-fishing rig
Sturgeon	4- to 8-inch nightcrawlers.	• Fixed or slip-sinker rig with 2 to 4 crawlers gobbed onto plain hook
Bullheads	Garden worms, red wigglers, leaf worms and other worms from $1^1/2$ to 4 inches in length; pieces of nightcrawler.	• Fixed or slip-sinker rig with 1 to 3 worms gobbed onto plain hook
Trout	Garden worms, red wigglers, leaf worms and other worms from $1^1/2$ to 4 inches in length; crawler pieces, whole crawlers (large trout).	• Split-shot rig and plain hook • In-line spinner tipped with worm • Small jig tipped with worm or half a crawler • Small float (fixed, slip or casting bubble), split shot and plain hook • "Cowbells" tipped with a worm

For panfish and other small fish that tend to nibble at the bait, hook a small worm several times, letting only about ½ inch of the tail dangle. A long-shank hook makes unhooking the fish easier because you can grab the hook more easily.

For trout or other fish that tend to "inhale" the bait, hook a worm through the middle so both ends dangle for maximum action.

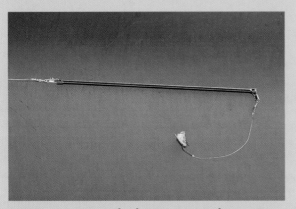

Lower a worm to the bottom on a "hanger" rig, which consists of a metal rod and an 8- to 12-inch dropper with a plain hook. You can also bait the rig with a minnow head. Bounce the rig on the bottom to "mud up" the water and attract perch.

Gob several worms (or crawlers) onto the hook to create a writhing mass that appeals to bullheads, catfish and sturgeon. Add new worms as needed to keep plenty of exposed ends wiggling. Some catfish anglers prefer treble rather than single hooks.

Add a single garden worm, red worm or leaf worm to a "cowbell" rig consisting of a series of large spinner blades. Cowbells, also called "pop gear" or lake trolls, are extremely popular among trollers because they produce flash that can be seen for a great distance in clear-water trout lakes.

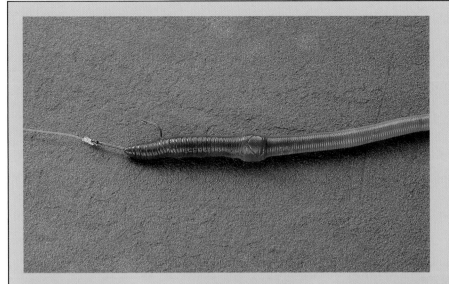

Walleyes and bass often favor the natural look of a nightcrawler hooked through the head. To make the worm trail straight without spinning, push a short shank hook into the tip of the head and out the side about ¼ to ⅜ inch back from the tip.

Use a "worm blower" to inflate a nightcrawler and make it float up off the bottom where fish can see it more easily. Insert the needle just behind the collar and squeeze a small bubble of air into the head. Inflating the tail makes the worm look unnatural.

Rig up a half crawler when the fish are striking short. For best results, hook the crawler through the broken end as shown. Most anglers report better success with the head section than the tail section but either will work.

Hook a nightcrawler onto a 2- or 3-hook worm harness to reduce the number of short strikes. When hooking the worm, remember that it will contract when you handle it, so you must leave a little slack between the hooks. This way, the worm can stretch out naturally without being restricted by the harness.

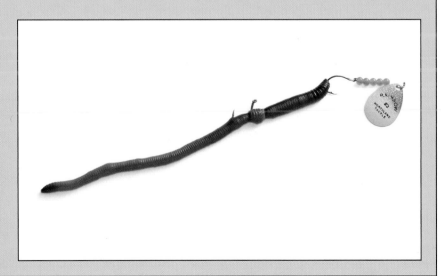

LEECHES

*E*ven the fussi-
est gamefish
find it hard to
resist a leech
squirming right
in their face.

LEECH BASICS

Biologists who study the food habits of freshwater gamefish know that leeches are a common item in the diets of many fish species. Yet leeches are nowhere near as popular as other common food items as fishing bait.

In the last few decades, leeches have gained popularity among walleye, sunfish and smallmouth bass anglers throughout much of the Midwest, and many consider them the premier bait for these species. But they have not caught on to that degree in other parts of the country, probably because many anglers consider them "bloodsuckers" and are reluctant to handle them.

In truth, the popular bait leeches are not bloodsuckers; they feed on small worms and other aquatic organisms, but they will not bore

ature, they tend to curl up into a tight ball and refuse to swim. The warmer the water, the more active a leech becomes.

Whether you buy leeches or trap your own, it's important to know which species work well for bait and which do not (below).

Good Leeches

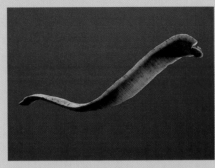

Ribbon Leech. *These common leeches may be brown, black, olive or mottled. Their body is firmer than that of a horse leech and the crosswise grooves are less distinct. They range in length from 2 to 6 inches when stretched out.*

Tiger Leech. *Much less common than the ribbon leech, the tiger leech is one of the most active leech species. Tiger leeches, which usually measure 2 to 4 inches in length, get their name from the 4 parallel black stripes on their back.*

Bad Leeches

Horse Leech. *Ranging in length from 3 to 12 inches, horse leeches may be black or mottled brown. They have very distinct grooves, a "squishy" feel and a powerful sucking disk that enables them to crawl out of a bait bucket.*

Medicine Leech. *Once used for sucking blood from sick humans, medicine leeches are easy to identify because of the row of red spots down the back and their rust-colored belly. Like horse leeches, they have a squishy feel and distinct grooves.*

through the skin of live animals to suck their blood. When a bait leech attaches to your skin with the powerful suction cup on its tail (wide end), it is only trying to hold on, not suck your blood. The mouth is actually located on the narrow end.

As a rule leeches work best at water temperatures of 50°F or higher. Below that temper-

COLLECTING LEECHES

If you live in an area with plenty of shallow, fertile ponds or "duck marshes," chances are you have a good supply of bait leeches available for easy harvest. Ponds inhabited by gamefish, however, seldom hold good populations of bait leeches. The fish eat them up!

Leeches are dormant in winter. But once the water temperature warms to about 50°F in spring, they become active and begin to swim about in search of food, making them vulnerable to trappers.

You can catch some leeches simply by walking around the edge of a pond, turning over rocks and logs, but you'll catch a lot more by learning the most productive trapping techniques.

By far the most common method is setting out coffee cans baited with fresh fish carcasses. Another effective technique is tossing out a gunnysack baited with fish carcasses, fresh beef, kidneys or liver. Leeches will even attach themselves to boards smeared with fish oil.

Ribbon leeches have a 2-year life cycle, spawning at the end of their second summer and then dying. This explains why the large leeches, called "jumbos," are nearly impossible to find in late summer, but smaller leeches are still available.

If you have purchased or collected jumbo leeches earlier in the year, however, you can keep them alive well into the fall simply by storing them in cold water (p. 73). This prevents them from maturing and then starting to spawn.

Using Coffee-Can Traps to Catch Leeches

1 Make leech traps out of 3-pound coffee cans. Attach a string and piece of Styrofoam to mark the trap's location. Weight the trap with rocks, bait it with fresh fish carcasses and pinch the top to keep out light.

2 Set the traps around sunset. Be sure they are completely covered with water, preferably in a spot where wind-induced current can spread the smell of the bait.

3 Pick up the traps before the sun comes up and drives leeches out of the trap. Pour the leeches into a bucket perforated with very small holes that will not allow the leeches to escape.

Using Gunnysack Traps to Catch Leeches

1 Put fish heads, fresh beef or other bait into a gunnysack, tie it shut with a rope and toss it into the water. Leeches will wiggle through the mesh to get at the bait.

2 Pull in the gunnysack the next day and open it up to remove the leeches.

KEEPING LEECHES

The secret to keeping leeches alive for long periods of time is refrigerating them at temperatures of 45°F or below. Cool temperatures keep them in a state of near dormancy so they do not require food and will not start spawning. A water temperature of 55°F or higher will trigger the spawning process, eventually leading to their death.

It's also important to keep your water clean and fresh. Be sure to change the water every few days, replacing it with well water or dechlorinated tap water of about the same temperature.

If you buy a few dozen leeches for a day of fishing and don't care about keeping them alive once the trip is over, you can keep them in a small lunch cooler, a Styrofoam bucket or even a flow-through bucket tied to your boat. But don't add these leeches to your home supply because they will soon die and contaminate the water.

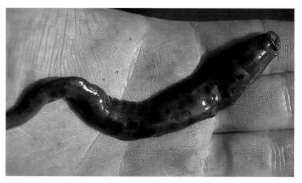

Discard any leeches that have red blotches; these hemorrhages are a sure sign that the leeches have started to spawn.

How to Keep Leeches Alive All Season

1 Refrigerate your leeches in a large plastic bucket or a cooler. A 5-gallon pail will easily hold 2 pounds of leeches. They don't require much oxygen, so there is really no need for a Styrofoam container.

2 Change the water every few days. If you're using city water, keep an extra bucketful in the refrigerator to dechlorinate it naturally before a water change is necessary.

3 When changing water, pour your leeches into a kitchen strainer or colander and remove the dead ones or any that have even the slightest growth of white fungus. If the dead or dying leeches are not removed, they will soon contaminate the water and kill the rest of your leeches.

How to Keep Leeches Alive on a Fishing Trip

Carry leeches in a lunch cooler or Styrofoam bucket. Keep the cover closed to prevent the sun from heating up the water. These containers, however, will not keep the water cold enough to delay spawning, so discard the bait when you're done fishing.

If you plan on adding the unused leeches to your home supply, keep your leech container inside a good-sized cooler with an ample supply of ice.

FISHING WITH LEECHES

If you've ever watched a leech swim through the water, you know why it makes such an irresistible target for many kinds of gamefish. A leech swims slowly, undulating wildly as it moves along, so all a fish has to do is leisurely cruise up to the morsel and inhale it.

But when a leech does not undulate as it normally would, it loses its near-magical attraction. That's why it's important to use hooking techniques that give the leech freedom of movement and to replace any leech that has been injured by nibbling panfish.

The importance of this intense action also explains why leeches work best in warm water. Northern anglers know that leeches are worthless as ice-fishing bait because they don't swim at all at near-freezing water temperatures. In fact, they usually wrap themselves around the hook, forming a hard ball. They will not swim normally until the water temperature rises into the 50s.

Even at warm temperatures, some leeches are more active than others. Savvy anglers spend some time sorting through their leech bucket, looking for the best swimmers.

Many fishermen make the mistake of using jumbo leeches that are more than 6 inches long when stretched out. These giant baits are sometimes referred to as "mud flaps." Although a good-sized fish won't hesitate to grab these baits, your hooking percentage may suffer. As a rule, you'll do better with a smaller leech that has an enticing action.

Popular Leech–Rigging Methods

Species of Gamefish	Size/Type of Leech	Popular Rigging Methods
Panfish (sunfish, rock bass, yellow perch)	Ribbon and tiger leeches from 1½ to 3 inches long (stretched out); pieces of leech.	• Small float (fixed, slip or casting bubble), split shot and plain hook • In-line spinners and small spinnerbaits tipped with small leeches • Plain hook and split shot fished on a cane pole or extension pole • Small jig tipped with piece of leech
Walleye and sauger	Ribbon leeches from 2½ to 5 inches long; tiger leeches from 2 to 4 inches long.	• Slip-sinker rig with plain short-shank hook or floater • Slip-bobber rig with plain short-shank hook or 1/16-ounce jig head • Split-shot rig and plain hook • Weight-forward spinner or spin rig tipped with leech • Bottom-walker rig with spinner and single hook
Smallmouth and largemouth bass	Ribbon leeches from 2½ to 5 inches long. Largemouth have been known to take 6- to 8-inch horse leeches.	• Slip-sinker rig with plain short-shank hook or floater • Split-shot rig and plain hook • Slip-bobber rig with plain short-shank hook or 1/16-ounce jig head • Spin-rig tipped with leech
Trout	Ribbon leeches from 2 to 4 inches long.	• Split-shot rig and plain hook • In-line spinner tipped with leech • Small jig tipped with leech • Small float (fixed, slip or casting bubble), split shot and plain hook

How to Hook Leeches

Through the tail. In most situations where you're retrieving the leech, hook it just ahead of the sucker on the tail.

Through the head. When nibbling panfish are stealing your bait, hook the leech through the tough skin of the neck.

Through the middle. When float-fishing or using any vertical presentation, hook your leech through the middle.

Select a lively leech by sorting through your bucket, looking for the most active swimmers. If you pick out a leech that wants to wrap itself around your hook, discard it and select a different one.

Should nibbling panfish injure your leech, causing it to lose its flattened shape, discard it and put on a new one.

Tip a tiny jig with a piece of leech to catch panfish. Any part of a leech will work, but many anglers prefer the head end because it is tougher. Hook the head section through the broken end.

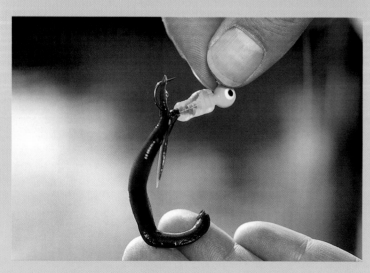

When tipping a jig, choose a fairly small leech and hook it through the head end. This way, it's more difficult for a fish to pick it off the hook and the leech is less likely to wrap itself around the lure.

Don't use leeches that are too large for the fish you're after. A leech that looks to be only 2 inches long in the hand may stretch out to a length of 6 inches or more in the water. An average-sized walleye or bass may grab a "mud flap," but it will probably strike short. A smaller leech is equally attractive and will significantly boost your hooking percentage.

When trolling with a spinner rig, choose one with a single hook rather than a 2- or 3-hook harness. This way the leech can wiggle more freely and won't wrap itself up in the harness.

Freeline a leech to catch walleyes, bass or panfish in shallow water. Just hook the leech ahead of the sucker with a short-shank hook, toss it out with light spinning gear and let it swim on its own.

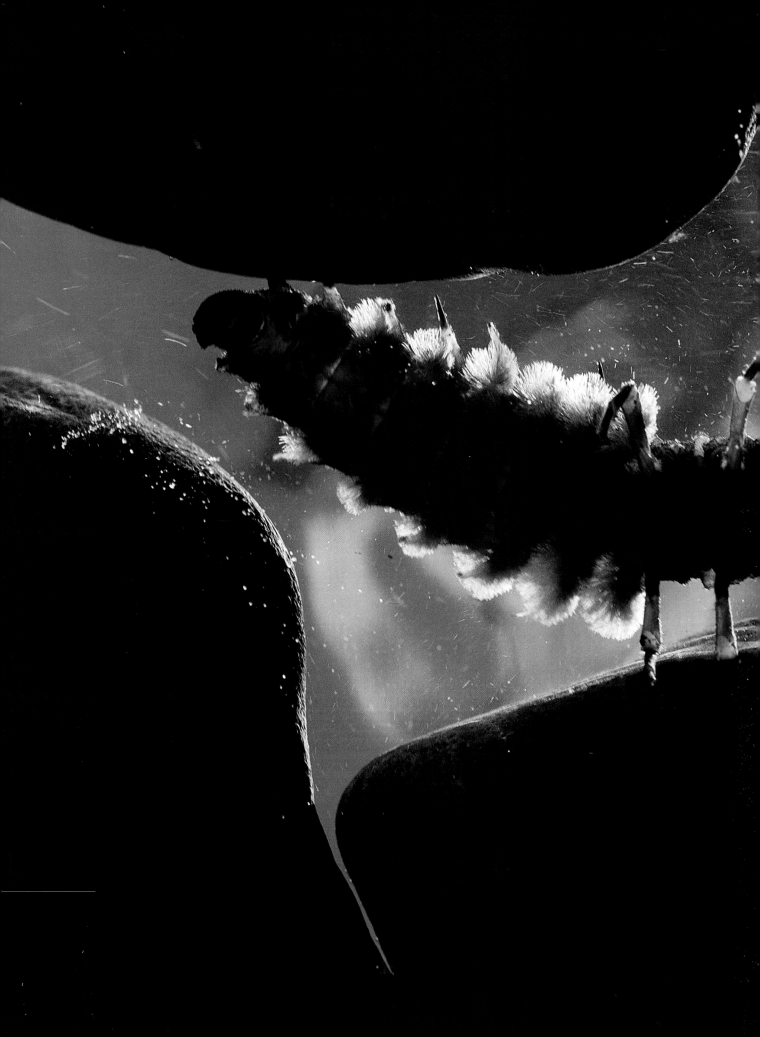

INSECTS

*P*ractically all kinds of gamefish feed heavily on insects at some point in their lives, so it's easy to understand why these delicate baits are so effective.

AQUATIC INSECTS

Every kind of freshwater gamefish habitat supports some type of aquatic insect and many waters hold hundreds of different types. Fly fishermen understand the importance of these insects more than other anglers, and have created a staggering array of fly patterns intended to "match the hatch."

Although there is a great deal of variation in aquatic insect life cycles, the cycle of the mayfly (below) is fairly typical. Like the mayfly, most aquatic insects have an immature stage that spends a year or more in the water. Their life as an adult, which lasts only a few days, is spent on land and in the air.

The immature forms of aquatic insects are much more widely used as bait because they're available throughout the year. They're also more appealing to gamefish and considerably easier to keep on the hook.

Despite the obvious appeal of aquatic insects to many kinds of gamefish, few anglers have taken the time to learn how to use live insects to their best advantage. On the following pages, we'll show you how to identify the aquatic insects most commonly used for bait, where and how to collect them and keep them in good condition, and the best techniques for using them to catch various kinds of gamefish.

Life Cycle of a Mayfly

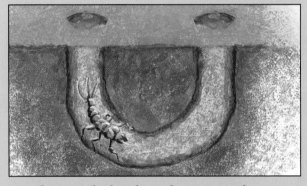

1 *Adult mayflies mate in flight and then the female deposits her fertilized eggs in the water. The eggs stick to plants, rocks and debris on the bottom.*

2 *The nymphs hatch in about 6 months. Burrowing mayflies (the largest types), tunnel into a firm mud bottom where they feed for several more months while undergoing numerous molts.*

3 *The full-grown nymph swims to the surface and sheds its skin. A dun or subimago, which has cloudy wings, then emerges and flies off to nearby vegetation where its wings can dry.*

4 *Within a day or two, the dun molts into a mature adult, called a spinner or imago, which has clear wings. The spinners deposit their eggs within a few days and then die.*

Mayflyies. *Often called "wigglers," mayfly nymphs (left) have a single pair of wingpads, gills on the abdomen and two or three long tail filaments. The adults or spinners (right), have clear, upright wings.*

Stoneflies. *The nymphs (left) have two pairs of wingpads, two short, thick tail filaments and gills on the underside of the thorax. Adults (right) are dull brownish or grayish and their wings lie flat rather than stand upright.*

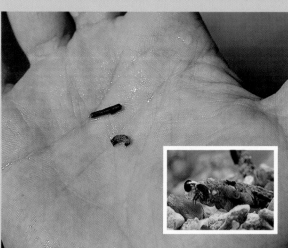

Caddisflies. *Caddisfly larvae or caddisworms (left) have a segmented, tan or cream-colored body with three pairs of legs near the front. Most live in a case made of sand or sticks, but some are free-living. The adults (right), are brownish and have tentlike wings.*

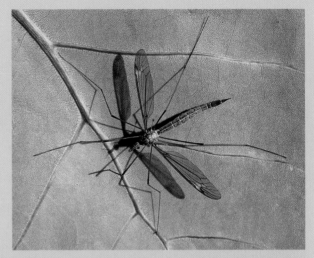

Craneflies. *Cranefly larvae, called waterworms (left), may be up to 2½ inches in length. The soft, segmented body is grayish or brownish and has several hairy projections on the tail. The adults (right) resemble giant mosquitoes.*

Dragonflies. *The stout-bodied nymphs (left) vary in color from dark brown to pale green. They can be identified by their large labium (lower lip) which is used to grasp prey. Adults (right) have a pair of large, usually multicolored, wings.*

Dobsonflies. *The larvae, called hellgrammites (left), measure up to 3 inches in length and have a forbidding look, with large pincers on their head. Adult males (right) may be as much as 5 inches long and have extremely long jaws.*

Large mayfly nymphs burrow into the muddy bottoms of streams and lakes where you can collect them with a larvae digger. Find an old pitchfork, remove the middle tines and attach some heavy wire mesh. Use the digger to scoop nymphs out of the mud.

COLLECTING & KEEPING AQUATIC INSECTS

Some bait shops periodically stock mayfly wigglers and possibly a few other kinds of aquatic insect larvae but, for the most part, you'll have to catch your own. Luckily, that's not too difficult if you know where to look.

If you live near a lake or stream, you'll periodically see hatches of adult aquatic insects, so you have a pretty good idea of what larval forms inhabit those waters.

If you don't have a nearby insect source, head for the closest trout stream if state regulations permit bait gathering on such waters. The cold, clear water usually supports a wide variety of insect life.

The secret to keeping aquatic insect larvae alive is keeping them in clean water at least as cold as the water from which they were captured. In many cases that means they'll have to be refrigerated. For a day of fishing, keep the larvae in a lunch cooler filled with damp moss.

Most types of larval aquatic insects require well-oxygenated water. If you keep them refrigerated, oxygenation is probably not necessary. But if you keep them in a cool spot in your basement, it's a good idea to aerate them using an aquarium pump and an air stone.

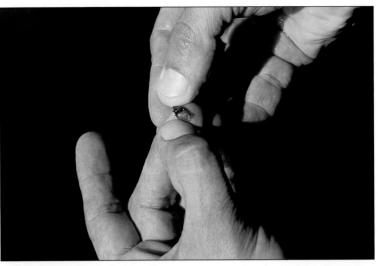

Pick caddis cases (the stone, stick or sand cases that house caddisworms) off the bottom of rocks found in cool- or coldwater streams (left). Break the cases open to remove the small worms (right). You can also find mayfly, stonefly and dragonfly nymphs clinging to the rocks.

Find waterworms by digging sticks, leaves and debris out of a muddy bank (left) or the upstream face of a beaver dam. Sort through the material by placing it into a wooden box with a bottom of ⅛-inch mesh screen (right) to find the larvae. You can also use the box to sort through leaves, sticks and roots of plants pulled from shallow water to find waterworms and other nymphs.

To catch hellgrammites and a variety of other larval aquatic insects, hold a fine-mesh net downstream of a rocky area in a stream while someone else turns over the rocks (left). The larvae will drift into the net and hellgrammites will grab the mesh with their pincers (right).

FISHING WITH AQUATIC INSECTS

Although larval aquatic insects are used primarily for trout, they're also popular for smallmouth bass, yellow perch and even walleyes. During a hatch, some anglers use the adult forms of mayflies and stoneflies, but these insects are extremely delicate and difficult to keep on the hook.

Even many of the larval forms are quite delicate, so it's important to hook them properly. Otherwise they'll fly off the hook when you cast, or nibbling fish will strip them off the hook.

Because of the delicacy issue, you should use a light-wire hook. If you attempt to push a heavy wire hook through the dainty body, you may damage the bait so it won't stay on the hook. If you're threading the bait on lengthwise, the hook should have an extra-

long shank.

A rod with a soft tip reduces the chances of losing the bait on the cast. Instead of "throwing" the bait, you can gently lob-cast it, letting the rod do the work and reducing the strain on the bait.

Popular Methods for Rigging Aquatic Insects

Species of Gamefish	Size/Type of Insect	Popular Rigging Methods
Yellow perch and walleye	Mayfly nymphs from 1 to 2 inches long.	• Small float (fixed or slip), split shot and light-wire, extra-long-shank hook • $1/8$- to $1/4$-ounce jigging spoon tipped with mayfly nymph • Jigging spoon with mono dropper and light-wire, extra-long-shank hook
Smallmouth and largemouth bass	Hellgrammites from 2 to 3 inches long; dragonfly nymphs from 1 to $1\frac{1}{2}$ inches long.	• Split-shot rig and plain hook • Fixed- or slip-bobber rig with split shot and plain hook
Trout	Stonefly and mayfly nymphs from 1 to 2 inches long, hellgrammites from $1\frac{1}{2}$ to 2 inches long, waterworms, 2 or 3 caddis larvae.	• Split-shot rig and plain hook • Small float (fixed, slip or casting bubble), split shot and plain hook

How to Hook Aquatic Insects

Mayfly Nymph. *Thread the nymph onto a size 10 or 12 long-shank, light wire hook. Most anglers thread the nymph head first, but some thread it tail first.*

Stonefly Nymph. *Hook the nymph under the collar using a size 8 or 10 light-wire hook.*

Caddis Larvae. *Hook 1 to 3 larvae through the head using a size 12 to 16 light-wire hook. Some anglers hook on the case and the worm.*

Hellgrammite. *Hook a hellgrammite under the collar with a size 4 to 8 light-wire hook. Grab it behind the head to avoid the pincers.*

Waterworm. *Push a size 8 or 10 light-wire hook through the tough skin just ahead of the projections on the tail.*

Dragonfly Nymph. *Hook the nymph under the collar using a size 8 or 10 light-wire hook.*

Tips for Fishing with Aquatic Insects

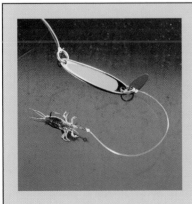

Make a dropper rig for yellow perch and walleyes by replacing the treble hook on a jigging spoon with a long-shank single hook on a 4- to 6-inch mono dropper. Thread on a mayfly wiggler.

Lob-cast delicate insect baits using a smooth sidearm motion. The rod tip must be soft enough to "load" on the backcast so the "recoil" can propel the bait on the forward cast.

TERRESTRIAL INSECTS

The term, "terrestrial insect" means any insect that completes its entire life cycle on land. Besides well-known adult forms like crickets and grasshoppers, many anglers use immature forms including caterpillars (butterfly and moth larvae), maggots (fly larvae) and grubs (beetle larvae).

Terrestrial insects are not a staple in the diet of most gamefish. In fact, few gamefish ever see the immature forms and they feed on the adults only on rare occasions in summer, usually when strong winds blow them into the water.

Nevertheless, terrestrial insects rank among the most effective baits for many kinds of gamefish. Although they are used most commonly for smaller fish, like stream trout and panfish, some types also work well for big fish. Catalpa worms, for example, are widely considered to be one of the finest catfish baits.

Common Adult Terrestrials

Grasshoppers. *There are hundreds of different kinds of grasshoppers, most of which inhabit grassy or weedy fields. They range in color from grayish to brownish to greenish. Those used for fishing are usually 1 to 2 inches long.*

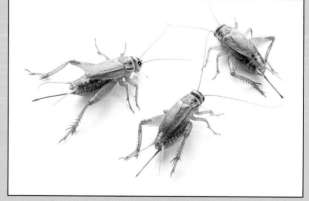

Crickets. *Gray crickets (shown) are grown commercially and are readily available at many bait shops or pet-supply stores. But anglers also use a variety of other crickets that they catch themselves, usually in grassy or weedy fields.*

Common Terrestrial Insect Larvae

Catalpa Worm. *These large worms (up to 3 inches long) are the larval stage of the catalpa sphinx moth; they feed on the leaves of catalpa trees. They have prominent black stripes down the back and a black spine on the tail.*

Waxworm. *Measuring from ½ to 1 inch in length, waxworms are larvae of the bee moth. They have a cream-colored body with distinct segments and a brownish head.*

Goldenrod Grub. *These small, whitish maggots, which are only about ¼-inch long, are the larvae of the goldenrod gall fly. They burrow into the stems of goldenrod plants, making the characteristic swellings or "galls."*

Mousee. *These small larvae, also known as rat-tailed maggots, are the immature form of the bee fly. Their tannish body is about ½ inch long, with a tubelike tail at least that long. They live in stagnant water and use the tube to breathe.*

Spike. *Housefly and blowfly maggots are often sold as "spikes" or "silver wigglers." Most varieties are light tan in color and measure about ½ inch in length.*

Eurolarvae. *Maggots of the European blowfly are fed dyed food and sold as "Eurolarvae." The tough-bodied larvae come in a variety of colors and are ⅜ to ½ inch long.*

Mealworm. *Commonly sold as "golden grubs," these inch-long larvae are the immature form of the darkling beetle. The yellowish to tannish body has distinct segments; the head is dark brown.*

COLLECTING TERRESTRIAL INSECTS

Most anglers buy their terrestrials from bait shops or pet stores, but it's possible to catch your own.

Collecting adult terrestrials is easy. You can net grasshoppers in a grassy field. Another good way to catch grasshopper is by hand on cool, dewy mornings when they are stil "stiff." Turn over logs to find crickets.

Some kinds of immature terrestrials, such as catalpa worms, are equally easy to find, but collecting other types can be a challenge and may even be dangerous or distasteful. You could, for example, collect waxworms by removing them from the cells of beehives, but there may be consequences. And you could easily gather spikes (maggots) from dead animal carcasses—if you don't mind the smell.

Here are the most common methods for collecting adult and immature terrestrials.

Collect grasshoppers by walking through a grassy field with a long-handled butterfly net on a warm summer day.

How to Collect Crickets

Turn over a log or board and then cover the insects with a net or coffee can (with the ends removed) to prevent them from escaping.

Sink a coffee can so the lip is even with the ground, bait it with bread crumbs and sugar, then place enough rocks around the rim to support a board that keeps out the rain. Crickets enter the trap at night; collect them the next morning.

Spread a sheet beneath a catalpa tree, then shake the branches to collect the catalpa worms. They're present from late spring to early fall.

Use a fine-mesh dip net to collect mousees from stagnant pools of water, such as runoff from live-stock feedlots or discharges from canneries.

Look for waxworms in the cells of neglected bee-hives. The worms tunnel into the cells to feed on the beeswax.

Look for mealworms in piles of rotting grain around silos, feed mills and grain elevators.

Collect galls from goldenrod plants from fall through winter. The plants grow in meadows, fields and woodland fringes. Discard any galls with holes in them; the worms have burrowed out or been eaten by birds.

RAISING TERRESTRIALS

Some of the most popular types of terrestrial insects, particularly waxworms and mealworms, are surprisingly easy to raise. Once you learn how it's done, you'll not only save money, but you'll also have a convenient year-round bait supply.

For some anglers, raising their own bait is just about as much fun as fishing with it. And bait "farmers" can often produce enough insects to supply most of their fishing friends.

Another advantage to raising your own: You'll never have to worry about the bait shop running out of your favorite offering, which is always a possibility when the bite is on.

How to Raise Mealworms

1 Supplies for raising mealworms include (1) ice-cream bucket with perforated lid, (2) wheat bran, (3) several 2- to 3-inch pieces of soft wood, (4) apples, (5) mealworms (for seed).

2 Fill an ice-cream bucket with a 2-inch layer of wheat bran (for food), then add a few pieces of wood and several dozen mealworms.

3 Place a few apple slices on top of the bran for moisture. Put the lid on the bucket and keep the bucket at room temperature. Replace the apple slices every few days so they do not rot. Potato slices will also work.

4 Within a few weeks, some of the mealworms will pupate and then emerge as beetles. The beetles mate and lay eggs in the bran or on the wood. The eggs hatch in about a week and, within several weeks, you can start harvesting the worms. One ice-cream bucket can produce 1,000 or more worms.

How to Raise Waxworms

1 Supplies for raising waxworms include (1) rice-based baby cereal (Pablum), (2) brewer's yeast, (3) honey, (4) glycerin, (5) beeswax, (6) 3-pound peanut-butter jar with screen lid, (7) wax paper and (8) waxworms (for seed).

2 Mix 14 ounces of cereal, 6 ounces of yeast and 2 ounces of grated beeswax in a large bowl. In a separate bowl, combine 6 ounces of glycerine, 7 ounces of honey and 3 ounces of water. Add the liquid to the cereal mixture and mix until it is moist.

3 Add the mixture to the jar and then put in a dozen waxworms. Place the screen lid over the jar and keep it in a dark place at room temperature.

4 When the waxworms start to spin cocoons at the surface of the mixture, insert a piece of pleated wax paper. This gives the moths a place to lay their eggs. Soon you'll see clumps of the whitish eggs clinging to the paper.

5 Within a few days, the eggs start to hatch into microscopic larvae. You can start harvesting waxworms within a month. One jar should produce at least 500 worms.

Commercial insect containers enable you to dispense crickets or grasshoppers one at a time without others escaping.

KEEPING TERRESTRIAL INSECTS

Whether you raise your own insects, collect them in the wild or buy them at a bait shop, you should know how to keep them alive. Most types will live for weeks or months if you keep them in the right medium and at the right temperature. Just check on them every few days and remove any that are sick or dead.

Anglers who fish with crickets or grasshoppers know that the insects are easy to keep alive, but if they're not kept in the right kind of container, some of them may escape when you're trying to grab one to put on your hook. Special insect dispensers (above) solve the problem.

Tips for Keeping Crickets & Hoppers

Keep crickets and grasshoppers at room temperature in an ice cream bucket with a perforated lid. Add a layer of grass or straw, some crumpled paper for cover and half a potato for moisture. If you'll be keeping the insects for more than 2 weeks, add a little cornmeal or rolled oats for food.

Before attempting to remove the insects for fishing, place the ice cream bucket in the refrigerator for about 15 minutes. This will slow them down enough so that you can transfer them to a dispenser without letting many of them escape.

Live Bait

Tips for Keeping Immature Terrestrials

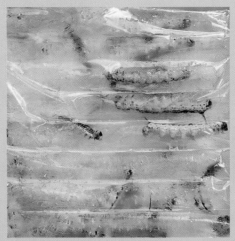

Catalpa Worms. *Keep catalpa worms and the large, heart-shaped catalpa leaves in a burlap bag (left). Store the bag in a cool, shady spot or in a refrigerator. If you need a year-round supply, freeze the worms in a small, resealable plastic bag filled with water (right). They freeze surprisingly well and retain most of their texture and color. Freezing them dry will make them mushy.*

Goldenrod Grubs. *Place unopened galls in a box and refrigerate them (left); the grubs will stay alive for several months. You can also remove the grubs by slicing the galls partway through, breaking them with your fingers (right) and then refrigerating the grubs in a small container of bran, cornmeal or rolled oats.*

Waxworms, Spikes, Eurolarvae, Mousees & Mealworms. *All these larvae can be kept in coarse sawdust or wood shavings in a pint- or quart-sized plastic container with a perforated lid (left). Mealworms should be refrigerated; the others can be stored in a dark spot at room temperature. Snuff boxes (below) make ideal fishing containers for all these larvae.*

FISHING WITH TERRESTRIAL INSECTS

For centuries, freshwater anglers have been catching fish on crickets and grasshoppers. And ice fishermen have long known that waxworms and other small terrestrial insect larvae are dynamite panfish baits. Until recently, however, these larvae were not widely used for open-water fishing.

Trout anglers, for example, are now discovering that larval terrestrials often work just as well as immature aquatic insects. And panfish anglers who previously swore by worms and small minnows have found that there are times when larval

baits work better.

One big advantage to larval baits: They seem to work better after fish have bitten them and broken the skin, releasing their body fluids. So there is no need to replace mangled bait; just add new bait as needed.

Popular Methods for Rigging Terrestrial Insects

Species of Gamefish	Type of Insect	Popular Rigging Methods
Panfish (sunfish, crappies, rock bass, warmouth, yellow perch)	Cricket, grasshopper, waxworm, mealworm, spike, Eurolarvae, mousee, goldenrod grub.	• Small float (fixed or slip), split shot and light-wire, extra-long-shank hook with cricket or hopper • Small float (fixed or slip), split shot and light-wire hook or tear drop with larvae • $1/16$- to $1/4$-ounce jigging spoon tipped with larvae • Jigging spoon with mono dropper and light-wire, extra-long-shank hook
Smallmouth and largemouth bass	Cricket, grasshopper.	• Split-shot rig and extra-long-shank hook • Insect floated on surface with extra-long-shank hook (no extra weight)
Trout	Cricket, grasshopper, waxworm, mealworm, spike, Eurolarvae, mousee, goldenrod grub.	• Split-shot and extra-long-shank hook with cricket or hopper • Split-shot and short-hank hook with larvae • Small float (fixed or slip), split shot and extra-long-shank hook with cricket or hopper or short-shank hook with larvae • Insect floated on surface with casting bubble and extra-long-shank hook
Catfish	Catalpa worm, grasshopper.	• Slip-sinker rig and plain hook • Slip- or fixed-bobber rig and plain hook • Plain hook on trotline

Grasshopper/Cricket. *Thread a grasshopper or cricket onto a light-wire, extra-long shank hook either (1) head first or (2) tail first. Trout fishermen often hook grasshoppers (3) under the collar with a light-wire hook for a more natural presentation.*

Spike & Eurolarvae. *These baits have very tough skin so they can be hooked lightly through the head with most of the body left dangling. Put 2 or 3 larvae on a light-wire hook or tear drop.*

Waxworm, Mealworm & Mousee. *Using a light-wire hook or tear drop, push the hook point through the head and out the side about ¼ inch down. The bait should hang straight down, not stick out to the side.*

Goldenrod Grub. *Put 2 or more of these tiny larvae onto a light-wire hook or tear drop. Push the hook through the middle of the body.*

Catalpa Worm. *Push the hook point into the back about ⅓ body length from the tail end. Bring the hook out the back midway up the body (left). Or thread the worm onto the hook tail first so the body lies straight (bottom).*

FROGS

*T*he number of frog-imitating lures on the market is testament to the tremendous fish appeal of these common amphibians.

FROG BASICS

If you hang around a north-country bait shop in the fall, you'll most likely hear the old-timers talking about the "frog migration." As the weather begins to cool, the frogs start moving from shallow marshes (that will soon freeze solid) to deeper lakes where they will hibernate in the muddy bottom.

Accordingly, that's the best time to toss out a lively frog to catch bass, walleyes, pickerel and other hungry predators patrolling the lakeshore for an easy meal as they try to fatten up for winter.

Decades ago, frogs were a much more popular bait than they are today. That's because modern anglers can buy a wide variety of soft-plastic frog imitations and many kinds of hard-bodied, frog-imitating topwaters.

Another reason for the

frog's declining popularity as bait: Widespread disease (particularly redleg disease) has decimated frog populations in many parts of the country. Wetland drainage and pesticides have also taken their toll as well.

Nevertheless, many experienced anglers know that a fake frog is no match for a live one kicking its way through the water. That explains why these anglers are willing to spend hours slogging along marshy shorelines with dip net in hand.

The leopard frog, by far the most common North American frog species, is also the most common bait species. But practically any kind of small frog can be used for bait. Surprisingly, tadpoles do not make good bait. It's not that fish won't eat them; they're just too delicate and nearly impossible to keep alive on the hook.

Bullfrogs, which may be more than a foot long, are rarely used as live bait, but they make good cut bait, especially for catfish.

Popular Bait Frogs

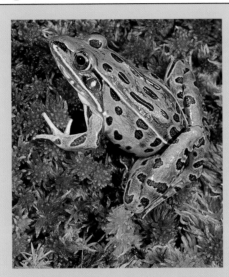

Leopard Frog. *The body is greenish to light brown with numerous irregular dark spots and distinct ridges running the entire length of the back. Leopard frogs measure up to 4 inches in length and are found throughout North America, with the exception of the West Coast.*

Green Frog. *These unspotted frogs, found in the eastern U.S. and southeastern Canada, vary in color from pale greenish to brownish and measure up to 3½ inches in length. They have ridges that extend from the head just past the middle of the back.*

Bullfrog. *These giant frogs are greenish to brownish with mottled undersides and no ridges on the back. The body, itself measures 4 to 6 inches in length, and the legs add another 7 to 10 inches. Bullfrogs are found throughout the U.S. with the exception of the Rockies and northern plains.*

CATCHING FROGS

You can start collecting frogs in early summer, as soon as they have emerged from their tadpole form. At first, they stay close to the waters from which they were hatched, so they're easy to find and collect. As they grow, however, they begin to scatter across the countryside. But you can still find them around marshy areas, wet meadows and lakeshores.

If you're able to pounce quickly, you can catch frogs by hand. But you'll prevent a lot of frustration and catch considerably more of them by using a dip net. Bullfrogs can also be caught by gigging or fishing with hook and line (p. 103).

The best time to collect frogs is in rainy weather, especially on rainy nights. They're less likely to move about when it's hot and sunny.

On a rainy night, look for frogs along roads with water on both sides.

Where to Find Frogs

Wet meadows make ideal frog habitat. Look for meadows that stay wet all summer rather than those that hold water only after a heavy rain.

Look for frogs along marshy shorelines of lakes and streams. They prefer a gradually sloping bottom with plenty of emergent vegetation.

How to Catch Frogs

Dip net frogs while walking along marshy shorelines or through wet meadows. Or dip net from the bow of a boat while your partner poles you through a shallow, weedy area. The ideal dip net has a 14- to 18-inch hoop, a handle at least 4 feet long and ¼-inch nylon mesh. If you're hunting at night, wear a headlamp; it will not only help you see the frogs, it will blind them as well, and keep your hands free to work.

Gigging, or spearing, is a good way to take large frogs that will be used as cut bait. Frog gigs are 3 to 5 inches wide with several barbed tines.

Catch bullfrogs or other large frogs by dangling a brightly colored yarn fly in their face at night. Frogs mistake the fly for an insect.

A fiberboard frog box has a slitted rubber top so you can reach in to grab a frog without the others jumping out. To keep the frogs moist, periodically dip the box into the water to soak the fiberboard.

KEEPING FROGS

You can easily keep frogs alive for a day of fishing or store them for a few days in a fiberboard or wire-mesh frog box or Styrofoam bucket. But if you want to keep them for weeks or months, you'll need a cooler or other large container that gives them more room. If crowded, they tend to become stressed and subject to disease. They'll also need fresh water, food, cover and a resting perch.

Always keep frogs at room temperature or a little cooler. They'll die quickly in warm weather if left in a container with no water. Don't make the mistake of putting too much water in the container, however. If frogs are forced to keep swimming, they'll soon weaken and die.

For long-term storage, keep frogs in a good-sized cooler with about an inch of water on the bottom. Add a few rocks and boards to provide resting perches and places to hide. Every few days, feed the frogs some crickets or other insects, and change the water once a week. Kept this way, frogs will live for months.

How to Make a Wire-Mesh Frog Box

1 Make a wooden frame out of 1 x 2s and staple ¼-inch wire mesh to all sides. Cut an 8-inch-diameter hole in the top.

2 Cut a 6-inch-diameter hole in a piece of ½-inch plywood, staple a piece of heavy rubber to the bottom and screw the plywood to the wooden frame. Cut a slit in the rubber for your hand. When fishing in hot weather, keep the box inside a cooler.

Tips for Keeping Frogs

Line your container with soft nylon mesh to prevent the frogs from jumping into the sides and injuring themselves. After the frogs become accustomed to the container, they'll calm down so the mesh can be removed.

If you don't have a slit-top frog box, keep your frogs in a minnow bucket filled with about 2 inches of water. This way, the frogs won't jump out when you open the bucket because they don't have a solid surface to push against.

Use a stout cane pole or extension pole to dabble a frog into openings in the vegetation. Dabbling enables you to place the frog exactly where you want it and, because you can set the frog down gently, it stays livelier than it would if you were casting.

FISHING WITH FROGS

A frog kicking its way through a shallow weedbed has a short life expectancy. The surface disturbance is almost sure to attract hungry gamefish.

Most anglers think of frogs as good bait for largemouth bass, but they work equally well for smallmouth. They're also effective for northern pike, pickerel and even catfish.

Frogs will catch fish most any time, but they seem to work best in fall. Some anglers claim that gamefish move into the shallows in fall to feed on frogs migrating from shallow marshes to deeper lakes. But it's more likely that the fish are in the shallows to gorge themselves on baitfish in preparation for winter, and they just happen to encounter the frogs.

Here are some things to keep in mind when using frogs for bait:

• Frogs are more delicate than you may think. Repeated casting will weaken or kill them. Always cast with a gentle, sidearm lob so the frog doesn't splash down too hard.

• Replace your bait frequently. When a frog tires and stops kicking, it is much less effective.

• Hooking fish may be difficult when using frogs. If you're missing too many fish, switch to a smaller frog and wait longer before setting the hook.

Popular Frog-Rigging Methods

Species of Gamefish	Size/Type of Frog	Popular Rigging Methods
Largemouth bass, smallmouth bass, walleye	Leopard frog or green frog no more than 3 inches long.	• Slip-sinker rig with plain or weedless hook • Split-shot rig with plain or weedless hook • Freelining or dabbling with plain hook and no extra weight
Northern pike, pickerel	Leopard frog or green frog no more than 4 inches long.	• Slip-sinker rig with wire leader and plain or weedless hook • Split-shot rig with wire leader and plain or weedless hook
Catfish	Large leopard frog or pieces of bullfrog.	• Large slip-float rig with plain hook • Slip-sinker rig with plain hook • 3-way-swivel rig with plain hook

Tips for Rigging & Fishing Frogs

Hook a live frog through the lips with either a (1) plain hook or weedless hook. When float fishing or freelining, you can also hook a frog (2) through the hind leg.

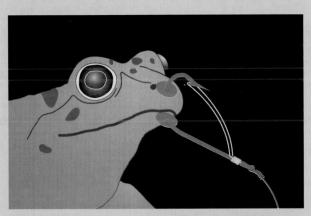

Keep a frog on the hook with plastic tabs punched from the lid of a coffee can. Push one tab onto the hook bend, hook the frog through the lips, then secure it with another tab.

Freeline a frog by feeding line as it swims over the vegetation. Keep your line taut, but not tight, so you can get a solid hookset when a fish strikes.

SALAMANDERS

*T*hese tough, lively amphibians have long been the "secret weapon" of Southern bass anglers.

SALAMANDER BASICS

Flip through the pages of your latest fishing tackle catalog and you'll see dozens of soft-plastic "lizards" and maybe a few "waterdogs." The popularity of these sala- mander imitations—and their real-life counterparts—stems from the common belief that salamanders are "nest rob- bers," so fish are quick to attack them to protect their eggs and young.

Live salamanders have long been a favorite of Southern bass anglers, but are used much less commonly in the North. They are popular,

may live on land or in the water, depending on the species.

Both adult and larval salamanders are used for bait. The most popular types fall into the 3 categories discussed here.

MOLE SALAMANDERS

These reclusive salamanders get their name from their habit of living in the underground tunnels of moles and other small mammals.

In spring, the adults emerge from the tunnels and migrate to small, fishless ponds to breed. The young reach full size by fall and then leave the water to begin their life as land-dwelling adults.

By far the most common mole salamander species is the tiger salamander (below).

Adult Tiger Salamander. *These large salamanders range from 6 inches to more than a foot in length; most anglers use 6- to 8-inchers for bait. Several species of tiger salamanders, all which have a distinctive yellow and black coloration, are found in the United States, southern Canada and northern Mexico.*

Larval Tiger Salamander. *Often called "waterdogs," larval tiger salamanders are generally considered to be much better bait than the adults. Waterdogs have external gills, tiny legs and a long fin extending around the rear of the body. They range in length from 4 to 8 inches.*

however, among some north-country anglers who target trophy walleyes and northern pike.

Although anglers refer to some kinds of salamanders as "lizards," they are amphibians, not reptiles. Most salamanders have an aquatic larval form, but the adult form

LUNGLESS SALAMANDERS

This is by far the most common salamander group, with almost 100 species found in North America. As their name suggests, they do not have lungs; instead, they absorb oxygen through their skin.

Anglers refer to some members of this group as "spring lizards" because they're commonly found in the vicinity of springs, brooks or small streams. Other types live in damp woodlands, taking cover under rocks or logs or burrowing into leaf litter and other debris on the forest floor.

Lungless salamanders have sleek bodies and are good swimmers, accounting for their popularity as fishing bait. Most anglers prefer the adult form.

Spring Salamander. The back and sides of the spring salamander are grayish to brownish with rows of darker spots that end at or above the legs. Adults range in length from 5 to 6½ inches. During the day, these salamanders hide beneath pieces of rock or wood in caves or along the banks of streams or springs. They can often be found feeding along stream-banks on rainy nights.

Dusky Salamander. The back of the dusky sala-mander is yellowish-brown to dark gray, sometimes with an irregular dark lateral band. Averaging just under 5 inches in length, dusky salamanders are normally found along the banks of springs and streams. They prefer moist soil but can survive in tiny, leaf-filled trickles and even in creek beds that are practically dry.

Redback Salamander. As their name suggests, redback salamanders have a reddish dorsal stripe. The back is dark gray to black and the belly is mot-tled with black and white. These small salaman-ders range from 2½ to 5 inches in length. They're normally found under rocks, logs and leaf litter in damp deciduous, evergreen or mixed forests.

GIANT SALAMANDERS

This group of large salamanders includes some species that reach more than 2 feet in length. The hellbender, for example, grows to a length of 30 inches and is capable of inflicting a painful bite. The giant salamanders used for bait, however, are generally no more than 12 inches long. Some giant salamanders take several years to mature, so it's possible to find bait-sized individuals even in waters inhabited by the larger species.

Giant salamanders differ from other kinds of salamanders in that they spend their entire life in water. Most have external gills that persist through life. One type, the siren (below), looks more like an eel than a salamander because it has only tiny front legs and no hind legs.

Siren. Found mainly in the coastal plain of the southeastern and south-central U.S., sirens favor the quiet, weedy waters of shallow ditches, swamps and ponds. Sirens vary in color from black to olive-green. The lesser siren ranges in length from 6 to 15 inches, but the greater siren (shown) has been known to reach lengths exceeding 3 feet.

Mudpuppy. These common amphibians have a broad head, thick body and paddlelike tail. The common mudpuppy (shown), found mainly in large, sluggish rivers, reaches lengths of nearly 20 inches. The dwarf mudpuppy has a slate-gray to purplish-black back with a few small, lighter spots and is $4\frac{1}{2}$ to $7\frac{1}{2}$ inches long. Dwarf mudpuppies are found in small, sluggish streams, mainly in coastal areas.

CATCHING SALAMANDERS

In some parts of the country, you can buy salamanders at bait shops or roadside stands. But they're not always available when you want them, so it's a good idea to learn how to catch your own.

Collection methods vary considerably, depending on the type of salamander:

Mole Salamanders

The best time to collect adult mole salamanders is on a rainy spring night, when they leave their burrows and migrate to their breeding areas. After dark, it's not uncommon to see hundreds of them crossing roads to get to the shallow, fishless ponds and ditches where they will breed. Once breeding has been completed and the adults return to their burrows, catching them is nearly impossible.

By midsummer, the larval salamanders have grown to a size where they make good bait. Then they can easily be seined in small ponds.

Lungless Salamanders

You can collect "spring lizards" by walking along the banks of small, coolwater streams after dark, using a flashlight or headlamp to spot the secretive amphibians crawling amongst streamside rocks and logs. They'll also hide under clumps of moss along the streambank.

To catch woodland salamanders, just turn over logs, bark or other debris on the forest floor. Or sort through leaf piles.

Giant Salamanders

Mudpuppies are most commonly caught by seining in slow-moving rivers, backwaters and canals, but you can also catch them on hook and line, using a small piece of worm for bait.

Look for sirens in shallow, weedy lakes, ponds and ditches. One way to catch them is by pulling up clumps of water hyacinth and shaking them into a screen box. But the best way to collect sirens is to wait for a heavy rain to draw them into ditches connected to shallow lakes and then catch them with dip nets or unbaited minnow traps (p. 116).

Tips for Catching Salamanders

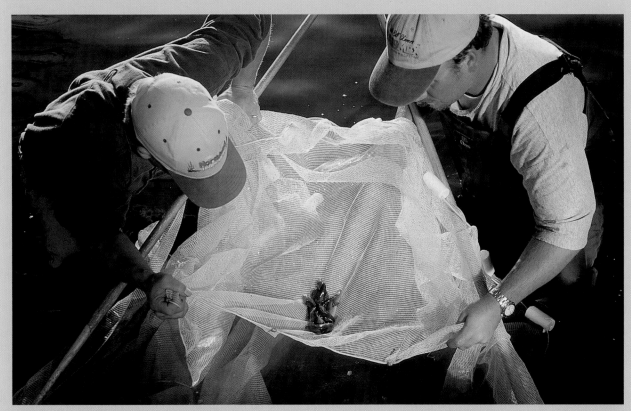

Collect waterdogs and mudpuppies using a nylon seine with ¼-inch mesh. To catch waterdogs, seine shallow ponds that dry up by late summer. For mudpuppies, try quiet lakeshores or river backwaters with sparse vegetation.

After a nighttime rain, look for spring lizards in window wells. As they're crawling about at night, they fall into the wells and can't climb out because of the slippery sides.

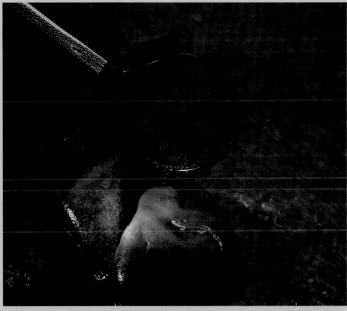

Collect spring lizards along rocky streambanks at night using a headlamp to spot them and a dip net to catch them. Spring lizards are very fast, so it's difficult to catch them by hand.

Turn over logs, pieces of bark, flat rocks and other debris in forested areas to find woodland species of lungless salamanders and sometimes mole salamanders. Or look for them moving about on the forest floor at night.

After a heavy rain that causes ditches, canals and other lake inlets to rise, collect sirens by dipnetting in the downstream side of a culvert or other obstruction that blocks their upstream movement (left). Or set an unbaited minnow trap in the same locations (right).

KEEPING SALAMANDERS

Most kinds of salamanders are surprisingly easy to keep alive. How you keep them, however, depends on whether they are aquatic or terrestrial.

This means that larval salamanders and giant salamander (larval and adult) should be kept in water. Other adult salamanders can be kept in damp moss, leaves or loose soil.

Salamanders can live for a month or two without food. But if you plan on keeping them longer, feed them worms, minnows or insects.

Keep terrestrial salamanders in a container filled with damp moss or leaves. Mole salamanders can also be kept in damp, loose soil. If the container is airtight, punch holes in the lid. Refrigerate it at a temperature of about 45°F.

Keep aquatic salamanders, with the exception of sirens, in cool water of about 50°F. Aeration is usually not necessary, but it's important to change the water every few days. A Styrofoam or plastic cooler makes a good container; it has plenty of bottom area so the salamanders can spread out.

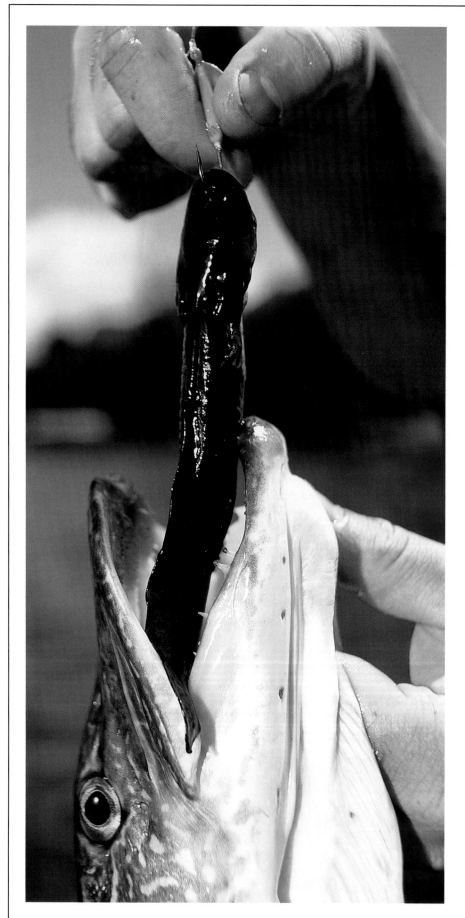

FISHING WITH SALAMANDERS

Innovative anglers throughout the country have discovered that salamanders are not just a bass bait. They also catch catfish, northern pike and even walleyes.

Big fish like big baits, so it's not surprising that large salamanders are considered prime fare for trophy fishing. An 8-inch waterdog, for example, makes an excellent bait for big walleyes and northern pike, and a foot-long siren is a premier bait for hefty largemouths.

Not all salamanders, however, are equally effective as bait. As a rule, the more active the salamander, the better fish like it. This explains why a waterdog, which swims with an enticing wiggle, usually works better than an adult tiger salamander, which swims lethargically or crawls along the bottom. Spring lizards are also active swimmers, but they tend to tire quickly.

Perhaps the liveliest salamander of all is the siren. Used mainly by bass anglers in the southeastern states, these snakelike amphibians swim with an irresistible motion unlike that of any other salamander.

The biggest problem in fishing with salamanders is getting a solid hookset. Fish tend to grab them by the tail and when you try to set the hook, all you get is a scuffed up salamander. To solve the problem, use smaller salamanders or rig them with a stinger hook (next page).

Popular Salamander-Rigging Methods

Species of Gamefish	Size/Type of Salamander	Popular Rigging Methods
Walleye, pickerel	Waterdog from 4 to 6 inches long.	• Slip-sinker rig with plain hook • Split-shot rig and plain hook
Northern pike	Waterdogs and "spring lizards" from 5 to 8 inches long.	• Slip-sinker rig with wire leader and plain or weedless hook • Split-shot rig with wire leader and plain or weedless hook
Largemouth bass, smallmouth bass	Waterdog from 4 to 8 inches long; adult salamander from 5 to 8 inches long (up to 12 inches for trophy largemouth).	• Slip-sinker rig with plain or weedless hook • Split-shot rig and plain or weedless hook • Freelining or dabbling with plain hook and no extra weight
Catfish	Waterdog from 5 to 8 inches long; adult salamander from 5 to 12 inches long.	• Large slip-float rig with plain hook • Slip-sinker rig with plain hook • 3-way-swivel rig with plain hook

Tips for Rigging & Fishing Salamanders

Hook a salamander through the lips, from the bottom up. If you're having problems keeping the bait on the hook, use plastic tabs as you would with frogs (p. 107).

Spring lizards and other adult salamanders are often hooked just in front of the back leg. Hooked this way, the bait stays alive longer and is not as likely to get off the hook.

Make a stinger-hook rig by tying a short length of mono to your main hook and then adding a size 8 or 10 treble. Push the treble into the body behind the rear legs.

When bass are in heavy weeds, freeline a siren by hooking it through the back as shown and then feeding line as it slithers through the vegetation.

CRUSTACEANS

*C*rustaceans may look for- bidding to anglers. But they're like candy to many kinds of gamefish.

CRUSTACEAN BASICS

Crustaceans are an important part of the diet of almost all gamefish, so it's not surprising that they make excellent bait. In the first months of their life, juvenile fish of all kinds feed on tiny planktonic crustaceans, such as water fleas. Later in life the fish eat larger crustaceans such as freshwater shrimp and crayfish. Here are the types of crustaceans most commonly used as bait:

CRAYFISH

More than 500 species of crayfish inhabit North American waters. They're found in every conceivable type of freshwater habitat including shallow, stagnant ponds, roadside ditches, natural and man-made lakes, fast-flowing coldwater streams and sluggish warmwater rivers.

Most fishermen don't attempt to distinguish one species of crayfish from another. The main consideration in selecting crayfish is size. Anglers targeting trophy largemouth bass use crayfish up to 4 inches long, while panfish anglers prefer those less than 2 inches long.

SHRIMP

Freshwater fishermen use both freshwater and saltwater varieties of shrimp for bait. Anglers in coastal areas can purchase live saltwater shrimp in bait shops or catch their own in coastal estuaries. They can also catch mud shrimp and ghost shrimp along the mud flats of estuaries. Inland anglers can buy chilled or frozen saltwater shrimp at grocery stores.

Several types of freshwater shrimp, called grass shrimp, are popular among panfish anglers. Saltwater varieties of grass shrimp are also used for bait.

River shrimp—large freshwater shrimp found in some major river systems—also make good bait. But their limited availability restricts their popularity to specific areas, mainly the lower Mississippi River region.

SCUDS

Fishermen commonly refer to these small crustaceans as "freshwater shrimp," but the term is a misnomer. Scuds are considerably smaller than true freshwater shrimp and lack the distinctive fanlike tail.

Scuds are found in a variety of freshwater environments ranging from small coldwater streams to shallow, fertile natural lakes.

Scuds are seldom sold at bait shops, but they're fairly easy to catch if you use the methods shown on p. 131.

When threatened, a large crustacean propels itself backwards with a flip of its powerful, fan-shaped tail.

Crustaceans Commonly Used for Bait

Crayfish. These large crustaceans have powerful claws, or pincers, and hard, thick shells. Most are brownish or greenish, but they may be reddish or bluish. Most species are 2 to 4 inches long when fully grown, excluding the pincers.

Saltwater Shrimp. Many species of saltwater shrimp, ranging from 3 to 5 inches in length, are used for bait. Saltwater shrimp have very small claws and short antennae and are tannish to pinkish in color.

Mud Shrimp. Found mainly on intertidal flats along the Pacific and Gulf coasts, mud shrimp have large pincers that resemble those of crayfish. They vary in color from pinkish to tannish to bluish and range in length from 4 to 7 inches.

Ghost Shrimp. These pale-colored shrimp are found mainly on intertidal flats along the Gulf coast. Ghost shrimp have one pincer that is considerably larger than the other, explaining why some anglers call them "one-armed bandits." They vary in color from pinkish to off-white and range in length from 4 to 7 inches.

Grass Shrimp. These diminutive shrimp, which are only 1 to 2 inches in length, have a light greenish to tannish color and a translucent, almost glassy look. Saltwater varieties are most common in estuaries along the Atlantic and Gulf coasts; freshwater types, in ditches, ponds and small lakes in the Southeastern U.S.

Scuds. Smaller than any other crustaceans used for bait, scuds range from ½ to ¾ inch in length. Unlike crayfish and shrimp, they do not have a fanlike tail. Scuds have the unusual habit of swimming on their side, explaining why they are sometimes called "sideswimmers."

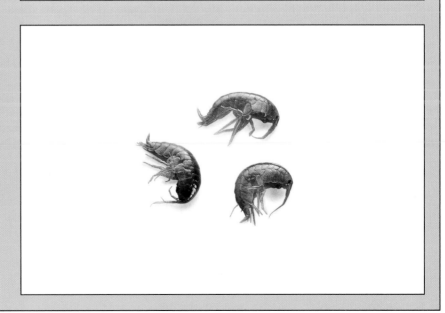

The quickest way to collect crayfish is to turn over flat rocks in a shallow, slow-moving stream and catch them by hand or with dip net. You'll have to be quick to catch them by hand; they'll scoot backward when you try to grab them.

COLLECTING CRUSTACEANS

There's no doubt that crustaceans make superb bait for many kinds of fish. But because their availability is limited, they are not as popular as many other kinds of live bait. In some states, the sale of crayfish has been banned as natural resource agencies attempt to prevent the spread of undesirable crayfish species, particularly the rusty crayfish (right).

Although most anglers have a pretty good idea of how to collect crayfish, they have little idea of where to find most other crustaceans, let alone how to catch them. On the following pages we'll show you where and how to collect the most popular types of crustaceans.

Rusty crayfish are native to streams in Ohio, Kentucky and Tennessee, but they have been spread throughout the Northeastern U.S. by anglers. They have a hard, thick shell with rusty colored spots on either side and large, powerful claws used for clipping off rooted vegetation. Rusty crayfish can wipe out the vegetation in a lake or stream, depriving gamefish of cover. If you encounter a rusty crayfish, do not transport it to another body of water.

Live Bait

Cruise along a rocky lakeshore of a clear lake after dark, using a powerful spotlight to find crayfish. Catch the crayfish using a long-handled, small-rimmed dip net. A larger net is not as maneuverable, so too many crayfish will escape.

Set a minnow trap in shallow, rocky areas of streams or lakes to catch crayfish. Bait the trap with a can of cat food punctured with an ice pick so the scent escapes slowly. You may have to slightly expand the entrance funnels so the crayfish can get in. Check the trap daily and remove the crayfish.

Catch crayfish on deep rock piles using a wooden slat trap. Bait the trap with a mesh bag full of chicken necks or fresh, cut fish. Crayfish will enter the funnel to get at the bait and, once in the trap, cannot escape. For best results, leave the trap out overnight.

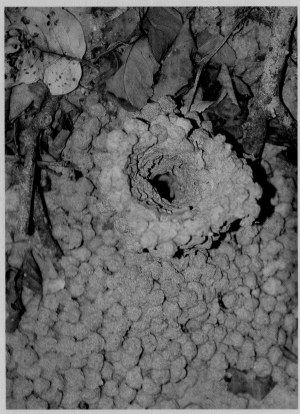

Look for the "mud chimneys" that mark the location of crayfish burrows. They're common along muddy lakeshores or streambanks. Crayfish leave their burrow on rainy nights and you can easily collect them by hand. A headlamp frees your hands so you can grab the crayfish more easily.

Use a pole-mounted coffee can with holes drilled in the bottom to catch crayfish crawling along the bottom. Hold the can behind the crayfish and poke the crayfish with a stick to make it scoot into the can.

Set an umbrella net in shallow water and bait it with chicken necks or fresh, cut fish. Attach a long handle to the net so you can lift it from a distance; otherwise, you may scare off the crayfish. Check the net after dark or in early morning.

How to Collect Saltwater Shrimp

Collect saltwater shrimp (and grass shrimp) by pulling a fine-mesh seine through grass beds on tidal flats. Seining also works well for collecting crayfish in streams. While two people stretch the seine across the stream, another kicks over rocks upstream of the seine. The crayfish dart downstream into the net.

Use a long-handled dip net to catch shrimp drifting through channels at night. Just stand on a low bridge or dock and shine a spotlight into the water. When you see the glowing eyes of a shrimp, maneuver the net to catch it.

Set a shrimp trap in a channel through which shrimp are drifting. Align the trap so the rectangular opening is facing directly into the current. Once the shrimp enter the trap, they cannot escape.

How to Collect Mud & Ghost Shrimp

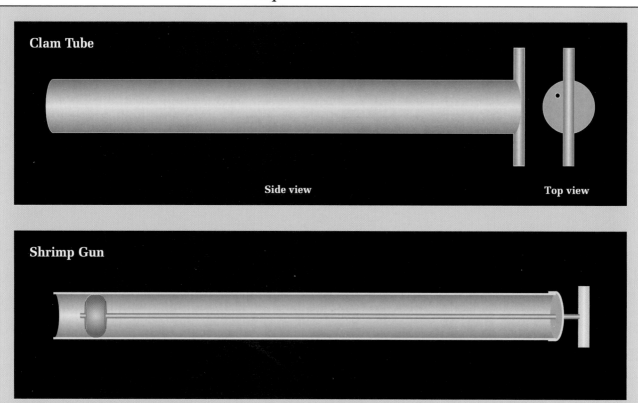

Wait until low tide and then collect mud shrimp or grass shrimp using a clam tube (top) or a shrimp gun (bottom). A clam tube is a 3- to 4-inch-diameter metal tube about 30 inches long with a handle and air hole on top. A shrimp gun is made from a 30-inch length of 3-inch-diameter PVC pipe. It has an end cap with a hole to accommodate a 3-foot, ¼-inch-diameter steel rod threaded on both ends. A wooden handle is attached to one end and a 3-inch rubber ball (compressed with washers and nuts) to the other. Just push the tube into the mud and pull the handle to extract the shrimp.

How to Use a Clam Tube

Place a clam tube over the entrance hole to a burrow; the hole is usually about 1 inch in diameter. Push the tube down as far as you can (left), then cover the air hole on top of the tube to create suction and pull the tube up steadily to extract the shrimp (right).

How to Collect Grass Shrimp

Dip net grass shrimp in eelgrass or other grass beds in tidal estuaries or in weedy areas of shallow lakes. Dump the contents of your net into a floating screen box so you can easily sort through the vegetation to find the shrimp.

To collect large quantities of grass shrimp, use a push net. Staple fine-mesh netting to a wooden frame from 18 to 36 inches wide, attach a handle and mount a roller just behind the front edge so you can easily push the device through grass beds.

How to Collect Scuds

Collect scuds in weedy streams or lakes by shaking clumps of vegetation into a pail or floating screen box. You may have to shake the weeds vigorously to dislodge the scuds.

Catch scuds in a lake using a fine-mesh plankton net. Some nets are designed to be cast with a fishing rod. Just toss the net into open water and retrieve it slowly; remove the bottle from the bottom of the net to collect the scuds.

Grab a crayfish across the back to avoid the pincers, which are surprisingly powerful.

KEEPING CRUSTACEANS

You can keep most types of freshwater crustaceans alive in cool, well-aerated water. Like fish, they extract oxygen from the water with their gills, so if you try to keep too many of them in a small, unaerated container, they will die from oxygen starvation. Warm water temperatures accelerate oxygen use.

Crustaceans differ from fish, however, in that they can also get oxygen from the air, as long as their gills are moist. This means that you can keep them alive by packing them in a bed of damp weeds.

The latter method works well for short-term storage of saltwater shrimp; but to keep them for an extended period, you'll need a saltwater live box (opposite). This is obviously not practical for most freshwater anglers, so they must settle for frozen or chilled shrimp.

When you collect crayfish, you'll notice that some of them have soft shells while others are very hard. The soft ones are those that have recently molted, and many fishermen believe softshells make the best bait. Normally, the shell hardens within a few days, but you can delay the hardening process as shown on the opposite page.

Grass shrimp can be kept alive in water but, should they die, the water quickly softens their bodies. Kept cool and dry (p. 134), they'll usually stay alive for a day of fishing. And even if they die, they'll still be usable.

How to Keep Crayfish

For long-term storage, refrigerate crayfish in a cooler or other good-sized container with just enough water on the bottom to keep their gills moist. Change the water every few days. As long as the craws are refrigerated, there is no need to feed them. For a day of fishing, keep them in a smaller cooler filled with damp weeds or moss.

Freeze fresh crayfish tails by placing them on a tray and then putting them in the freezer. Be sure the tails are separated so they do not freeze together (left). Once the tails are completely frozen, place them in resealable bags (right). Frozen this way, you can take only as many as you need for a day of fishing, rather than deal with a solid frozen block. Fresh saltwater shrimp can also be frozen this way, but grass shrimp tend to soften too much when frozen, so they are difficult to keep on the hook.

Alternate layers of damp newspaper and crayfish in a good-sized cooler and keep it refrigerated at a temperature of about 40°F (left). This method works well for keeping any crayfish, but is especially effective for keeping softshells (right) soft. The damp newspaper can delay the hardening process for as much as 2 weeks.

How to Keep Saltwater Shrimp

Saltwater shrimp can be easy to gather by hand at low tide. Keep them in a bait bucket (left) as you work, but get them to better storage quarters quickly—within an hour. Anglers in coastal areas keep large quantities of shrimp alive for long periods in a wire-mesh box sunk beneath a dock in a boat harbor or estuary. You can keep small quantities of shrimp in a regular flow-through bait bucket (right) suspended below a dock. To keep grass shrimp, you'll need a box with fine mesh or bucket with extra-small holes. Use a dip net to remove the shrimp.

For a day of fishing, put a layer of ice in a cooler and spread a layer of fresh aquatic vegetation over the ice. Add a a few dozen shrimp and cover them with another layer of vegetation.

Keep grass shrimp on a bed of newspaper in a lunch cooler with an ice pack in the lid. The shrimp will stay alive for hours and, even if they die, they'll still be firm enough to keep on the hook.

How to Keep Scuds

Keep scuds alive in a Styrofoam bucket stored in a cool spot. These tiny crustaceans do not require much oxygen, but if you want to keep a large quantity, you may have to aerate them with an aquarium pump.

For long-term storage, freeze scuds in an ice-cube tray (a dozen scuds per cube). When the cubes are frozen solid, remove them and keep them frozen in resealable plastic bags.

Another way to preserve scuds is to sun-dry them on a window screen (left). You may have to put another layer of screen on top to protect them from birds and small mammals. When the shells feel hard, put the scuds in small, resealable plastic bags (right) and freeze them for later use. This method also works well for preserving grass shrimp.

FISHING WITH CRUSTACEANS

Crustaceans have one big advantage over other kinds of natural bait: They emit a strong scent that attracts fish from a considerable distance.

Despite this fact, crustaceans, with the notable exception of crayfish, are not widely used among freshwater fishermen. They are extremely popular in certain areas, however, and their popularity is increasing as more and more anglers are discovering their virtues.

Here are some guidelines for fishing with each type of crustacean:

Crayfish

Although crayfish are widely known as an excellent bait for smallmouth bass, they also work well for largemouth bass, catfish and large trout, including steelhead. And small crayfish (less than 2 inches long) are an underrated bait for yellow perch, rock bass, shellcrackers, longear sunfish and even crappies. Peeled crayfish tails are another good option for panfish.

Although some anglers

insist that softshell crayfish catch more fish than hardshells, others say it makes little difference—as long as the crayfish is the right size for the fish you're targeting. A good-sized crayfish in defensive posture with pincers outstretched may look too intimidating for all but the largest gamefish.

Shrimp

Grass shrimp have long been a favorite of panfish anglers in Florida and other southeastern states. And their popularity is growing as they are being offered by more and more bait shops in other parts of the country.

The larger species of shrimp have not gained widespread popularity among freshwater fishermen, but anglers in coastal areas use them to catch largemouth bass, catfish, sturgeon, steelhead and salmon.

Scuds

Scuds are an excellent trout bait, as evidenced by the dozens of fly patterns intended to imitate them. Although they work equally well for panfish, few panfishermen have ever heard of them.

The main reason scuds are not more popular is their delicacy. Fish can easily pick them off the hook, and they may tear off when you cast. It helps to use small, light-wire hooks and lob cast with a soft-tipped rod.

Popular Methods for Rigging Crustaceans

Species of Gamefish	Size/Type of Crustacean	Popular Rigging Methods
Panfish	Scuds, grass shrimp, crayfish less than 2 inches long, crayfish tails, pieces of saltwater shrimp.	• Split-shot rig and light-wire hook • Slip- or fixed-bobber rig with light-wire hook or teardrop • Jig tipped with scuds, grass shrimp or pieces of shrimp
Largemouth bass, smallmouth bass	Crayfish from 2 to 4 inches long, shrimp from 3 to 5 inches long (primarily for largemouth).	• Slip-sinker rig with plain or weedless hook • Split-shot rig with plain or weedless hook
Catfish	Crayfish from 3 to 4 inches long, shrimp from 3 to 5 inches long.	• Slip-sinker rig with plain hook • 3-way-swivel rig with plain hook • Large slip-float rig with plain hook
Sturgeon	Mud shrimp and ghost shrimp from 4 to 7 inches long.	• Slip- or fixed-sinker rig with plain hook
Trout	Scuds, grass shrimp, crayfish no more than 3 inches long, crayfish tails.	• Split-shot rig and regular or light-wire hook • Slip- or fixed-bobber rig with regular or light-wire hook • Casting bubble with plain hook (scuds and grass shrimp)
Salmon, steelhead	Mud and ghost shrimp from 3 to 5 inches long. Crayfish up to 3 inches long (steelhead only).	• Slip-sinker rig with plain hook • Split-shot rig with plain hook • Surgical-tubing rig with plain hook • Fixed-bobber rig to float shrimp • Floating spinner tipped with piece of shrimp

How to Hook Crustaceans

Crayfish. *Hook a crayfish by pushing the hook through the bony "horn" on its head (left). Hooked this way, a crayfish is not likely to scoot backward, crawl under a rock and get you snagged. If the horn is too fragile, hook the craw through the side of the next-to-last segment of the tail (right). The latter method is also a better choice in very clear water, because the hook is less apparent.*

Crayfish Tail. *Push the hook into the broken end of a crayfish tail and bring the point out through the top of the shell.*

Grass Shrimp. *When fishing with a float, hook a grass shrimp through the back (left) so it hangs level in the water. To tip a jig, push the hook through the head and out the back (right).*

Saltwater Shrimp. *Hook a whole shrimp (1) through the tail, or cut it in half and hook it through the broken end with either a plain hook (2) or a jig (3). For panfish, hook a small piece of peeled shrimp onto a plain hook (4).*

Scuds. *Thread several scuds onto a light-wire hook (left) or teardrop (right) so that only the tails dangle. Inspect the bait often and add more scuds as needed.*

Tips for Fishing with Crustaceans

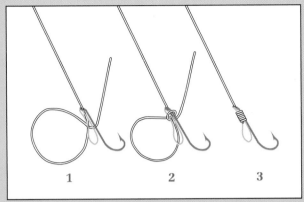 

Snell a rubber band onto a long-shank hook (left) to secure mud shrimp or other fragile crustaceans. Lay the rubber band on the hook shank then (1) push the line through the hook eye and make a loop in the line. (2) Wrap the free end through the loop and around the hook shank and rubber band; continue wrapping about 6 times. (3) Snug up the knot by pulling on the standing line and the free end. Then thread the middle of the shrimp onto the hook and then pull the rubber band over the tail (right).

Another way to keep fragile crustaceans on the hook is to thread them on as shown above and then wrap the tail with a piece of soft copper wire or a pipe cleaner.

To attract panfish or trout, mash a few dozen scuds in a small container and then dip a small jig with a hair, feather or soft-plastic tail into the juice so it absorbs the scent. Redip the jig frequently.

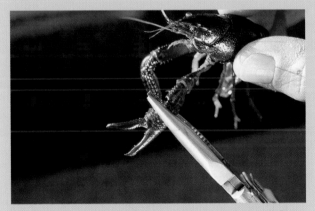 

Remove the pincers of a large crayfish to make it look smaller and less formidable. Using needlenose pliers, squeeze the claw firmly and it will neatly detach from the body without injuring the craw.

Use a float to keep a mud or ghost shrimp from dragging on a rocky streambed. It's difficult to keep these delicate crustaceans on the hook if they're allowed to tumble along the bottom.

POTPOURRI

*V*eteran anglers know that there are times when these unusual baits will greatly outproduce the standard offerings.

EGG BAITS

During the spawning run, salmon and trout gorge themselves on a natural food not present at other times of the year: Their own eggs. Normally, the eggs they eat are those that have drifted from their redds and have no chance to survive.

Serious fishermen know that eggs are a can't-miss bait for practically all species of trout and salmon. They work especially well during the spawning run, but will catch fish anytime. Some anglers rely on fake eggs and egg clusters, but these imitations are seldom as effective as the real thing.

Real eggs produce a strong scent that fish can detect from a considerable distance. Fresh eggs "milk" when dropped into the water, leaving a visible trail that clearly marks the path of the scent. When the eggs stop milking, it's time to put on some fresh ones.

Anglers use single eggs, egg chunks and spawn bags for bait (right). Any kind of trout or salmon eggs can be used, but the eggs of most trout are much smaller than those of salmon, so they are difficult to fish individually.

Egg chunks must be cut

Popular Types of Egg Baits

Single Egg. *An individual egg on an egg hook is an excellent bait for any kind of trout or salmon.*

Spawn Bag. *Wrap loose eggs in a piece of mesh that allows the scent to escape. Spawn bags work well for salmon and good-sized trout.*

Egg Chunk. *For salmon or large trout, cut a chunk from a fresh skein and push the hook through the membrane several times to secure the eggs.*

from a fresh *skein*, or egg sac. The membrane covering the skein is needed to keep the eggs on the hook. When the eggs mature, the membrane weakens and you'll need a spawn bag to hold the eggs together.

Whatever eggs you use, make sure they are clear and firm. Cloudy or mushy eggs have been dead too long and are seldom as effective.

Raiding garbage cans is not the most pleasant way to gather eggs, but it's highly effective.

COLLECTING & PRESERVING EGGS

When you're in trout or salmon country and you see someone rooting through garbage cans at the fish-cleaning station, don't feel sorry for them: They're just trying to find some eggs to use for bait.

During the spawning season, you may be able to buy fresh spawn at certain bait shops, but most anglers opt for the garbage-can method. Otherwise, you'll have to catch a spawn-laden female on an artificial.

If you're lucky enough to obtain a good supply of spawn, you'll probably have more than you need for the day's fishing. You can refrig-erate the eggs for a few days and they'll still be in good condition but, if you want to keep them longer, you'll have to preserve them (pp. 146-147).

Ask a successful angler if he or she can spare a few eggs to get you started. If the fish are biting, you shouldn't have any trouble finding a good egg supply.

How to Remove Spawn from a Fresh Salmon or Trout

1 Make a cut along the length of the belly to expose the egg skeins. The cut should be very shallow so you do not damage the membrane surrounding the skeins.

2 Carefully grasp the egg skeins and pull gently to free them. If they do not pull out with moderate pressure, cut the ends with a sharp knife.

3 Set the skeins on a bed of crushed ice in a cooler. Do not allow them to soak in water or they will milk out before you can use them. If there is any chance of them getting wet, put them in a resealable plastic bag.

How to Preserve Single Salmon Eggs

1 *Put some salmon eggs in a strainer and rinse them with cold water. Allow them to dry for an hour or two, until the shells look wrinkled.*

2 *Soak the dried eggs in a boric acid solution (1 tablespoon boric acid crystals per quart of water). Stir periodically until the eggs lose their wrinkles.*

3 *When the eggs feel firm and rubbery, drain them in a strainer and spoon them into a small jar. They will keep up to 6 months in a refrigerator.*

How to Preserve Spawn Chunks

1 *Dry a skein of eggs by wrapping it in paper towels and refrigerating it for 2-3 days.*

2 *Spread a layer of powdered, non-detergent borax on some newspaper and then cut the skein into chunks of the desired size. Leave the skein membrane intact.*

3 *Coat the egg chunks with borax to preserve them.*

4 *Add an inch of borax to a small jar, drop in the coated egg chunks and cover with an airtight lid. Shake the jar to thoroughly coat the chunks. They can be frozen or kept refrigerated for 2-3 weeks.*

How to Tie & Preserve Spawn Bags

1 Cut nylon mesh or a nylon stocking into 3-inch squares and then add chunks of spawn or loose eggs.

2 Gather the corners of the mesh to form a bag that measures from ½ to ¾ inch in diameter.

3 Using red or orange thread, make about 6 wraps around the tightly formed spawn bag.

4 Hold the wraps with your fingers so they do not unravel, and then tie several half-hitches around the bag.

5 Trim the excess thread and mesh.

6 Place the bags into a jar with a layer of borax and shake thoroughly to coat them. They can be refrigerated for 2-3 weeks or frozen.

RIGGING & FISHING EGG BAITS

Spawn bags and chunks are normally used to catch salmon and large trout, while single eggs work better for smaller trout. But a trophy chinook will pick up a single egg and a pan-sized rainbow will inhale a spawn bag that barely fits into its mouth. The main consideration in selecting egg baits is the type of water—not the type of fish.

For example, when you're drift fishing in strong current, a spawn bag is a better choice than a single egg or spawn chunk because the bag stays on the hook much longer. But when the stream is low and clear, a single salmon egg works better because of its natural look. A fresh spawn chunk is the best bet in slow or still water; it emits more scent than a spawn bag, yet stays on the hook fairly well.

Although drift-fishing while wading a stream is the most popular way to present egg baits, some anglers prefer to float-fish from a boat or fish with a fixed- or slip-bobber rig, either in still or moving water.

Whatever type of egg bait you prefer, be sure it's fresh. When the eggs start to look washed out, replace them. Washed out eggs emit very little scent and attract few fish.

How to Hook Egg Baits

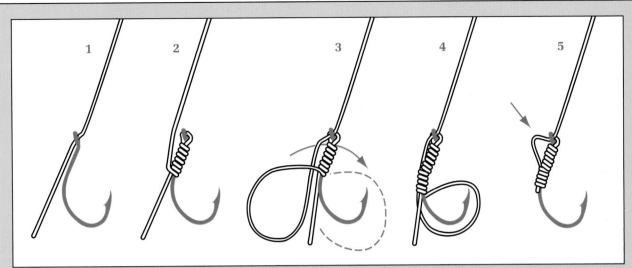

Egg Chunk. *To hold an egg chunk on the hook, make an egg loop. Using a hook with a turned up eye and a 2-foot piece of mono: (1) push your line through the eye; (2) make 6 wraps around the shank and tag end and hold the wraps with your fingers; (3) push the other end of the line through the eye, leaving a loop; (4) wrap one leg of the loop over the other leg and the tag end about 6 times, as shown; (5) snug up the knot by pulling on the line, then open the loop (arrow) by pushing on the line. Finally, cut a chunk of eggs from a fresh skein, put them into the loop and snug up the line.*

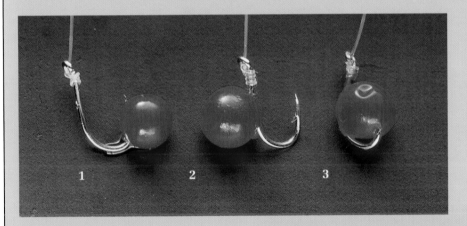

Single Egg. *(1) Push the hook through the side of the egg, (2) turn the hook 180 degrees and (3) bury the point in the opposite side of the egg.*

Spawn Bag. *You can tie a spawn bag as small as ³/₈ inch in diameter for stream trout or as large as ³/₄ inch for steelhead or salmon. Select a short shank hook that suits the size of the spawn bag and then push the point in one side of the bag and out the other, leaving the hook point exposed as shown. The hook eye should barely protrude from the bag.*

Drift-Fishing with Egg Baits

Add a pinch-on sinker or enough split shot to your line (inset) so your bait bumps naturally along the bottom at the same speed as the current. If you do not use enough weight, the current will lift your bait off the bottom; if you use too little, the bait will catch on the bottom and won't drift fast enough. Angle your cast upstream to (a) the closest part of a likely riffle or run. Hold your rod tip high as your bait drifts, keeping the line taut until the bait is well downstream of your position. Make several drifts through the same zone. Then reel up and make (b) a slightly longer cast at the same angle. Repeat the procedure until the entire riffle or run has been thoroughly covered (c and beyond).

Float-Fishing with Egg Baits

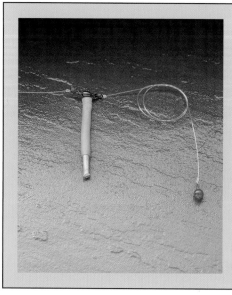

A surgical-tubing rig is ideal for float-fishing on a snaggy bottom. Just push a piece of pencil lead into the tubing. Then, should the pencil lead get snagged, it will pull out so you don't lose the whole rig.

Control the boat with oars or a small motor to keep it drifting at the same speed as the current. This way your line stays vertical, enabling you to easily feel the bottom and detect bites.

Tips for Fishing with Egg Baits

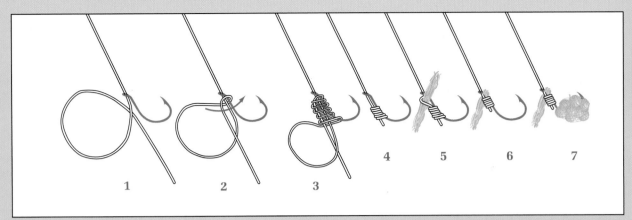

Snell a piece of yarn onto your hook for extra attraction. To make a snell: (1) push the line through the hook eye; (2) make a loop in the line; (3) wrap the free end through the loop and around the hook shank 6 times; (4) snug up the knot by pulling on the standing line and the free end; (5) insert a short piece of yarn under the standing line; (6) pull on the standing line until the snell abuts the hook eye. Finally, (7) push your hook into a spawn bag so the point is barely exposed.

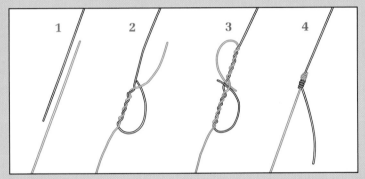

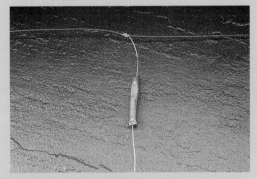

When drift-fishing on a snaggy bottom, use a dropper rig instead of pinching the sinker directly onto your line. To make a dropper, cut your line and then retie it using a blood knot (left): (1) Hold the lines alongside each other, with the ends facing opposite directions; (2) wrap one line around the other 4-5 times, and pass the free end between the two lines, as shown; (3) repeat step 2 with the other line; (4) pull on both lines to snug up the knot and leave one tag end untrimmed. Pinch pencil lead or split shot onto the dropper (right). When the sinker snags, a sharp tug will pull it off of the line and free the rig. Then all you have to do is pinch on a new sinker.

For a day of fishing, carry spawn bags or preserved egg chunks in a flip-top egg dispenser that attaches to your belt.

Thread a floater, such as a "corkie," onto your line before tying on your hook. A floater not only reduces the number of snags, it acts as an attractor. Some floaters are designed to spin for even more attraction.

FISHING WITH CLAM MEAT

Given the opportunity, many kinds of gamefish feed on clams and other molluscs. In fact, the shellcracker (redear sunfish) gets its name from its habit of eating small clams and snails.

Although clam meat is a favorite of some sunfish anglers, it is used more commonly by river fishermen in search of larger quarry, particularly catfish and sturgeon.

You can find clams in practically any body of unpolluted water. In clear lakes and rivers, all you have to do is wade through the shallows and pick them up. If the water is not clear enough to

see them, just take off your shoes and feel for them with your bare feet. They're most numerous on a clean, sandy bottom.

Clams are easy to keep alive. They'll live for a few days in a bucket of water kept in a cool spot, and for several weeks in a submerged live box.

The biggest problem in fishing with clam meat is keeping it on the hook. Although the meat is somewhat rubbery, it tears off quite easily, especially when you cast. But you can secure it just as you would fresh spawn, enclosing it in a mesh

bag or holding it on with a loop of mono. Gobbing it onto a treble hook also works well (opposite).

Most anglers use fresh clam meat. But for catfish you may want to try soaking the meat in sour milk for a few days. Catfish are attracted to the strong smell of spoiled clams and the soaking process firms up the meat.

Clam meat is usually fished on the bottom, using a fixed- or slip-sinker rig. But sunfish anglers and a few catfishermen prefer to suspend it from a float.

Pry open a live clam and look for the firm muscle, called the "foot" (arrow). This is the part that makes the best bait.

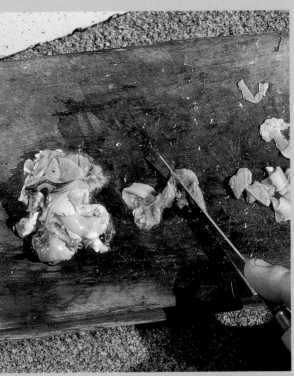

Save the rest of the clam meat, dice it into small pieces and then use it for chum. Spread it around your fishing spot at least ½ hour before you start fishing.

For sunfish, cut the foot into small pieces and push one or two of them onto a long-shank hook.

For larger fish, tie the meat into (1) a mesh bag or secure it with (2) an egg loop. Where legal, gob the clam meat onto (3) a treble hook, pushing each barb through the meat.

FISHING WITH BLOOD BAIT

Many catfish experts swear by blood bait, especially for catching channels and blues. Blood bait leaves an intense scent trail, drawing catfish from a long distance.

You can make blood bait from the blood of most any warm-blooded animal, but most anglers use beef or chicken blood because it's readily available at slaughter houses and processing plants.

Most anglers still-fish with blood baits, waiting for the scent to draw catfish. This technique works best in big rivers and reservoirs that have enough current to create a scent trail.

In still waters, blood baits are effective when bumped along the bottom from a drifting boat. Catfish combing the bottom for food are quick to detect the scent trail and follow it to your bait.

You can buy prepared blood baits, but most serious catfishermen prefer to make their own using fresh blood. Some anglers use chicken or beef liver instead of blood. These baits, when fresh, also emit a bloody scent trail but it is less intense than that of pure blood.

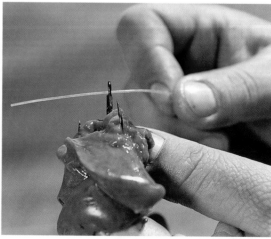

Push some liver over the shank of a treble hook, impale it onto the 3 points and then tie your line to the hook.

How to Make Blood Bait

1 Obtain some fresh blood from a slaughterhouse and pour it into a large baking pan at least 1 inch deep.

2 Refrigerate the pan for about 5 days or until the blood congeals into a firm, rubbery mass.

3 Set the pan in the sun for a few hours until the blood forms a tough skin, which helps keep it on the hook. Then cut the bait into 1- to 3-inch squares and refrigerate them in resealable plastic bags.

How to Hook Blood Bait

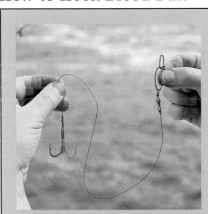

1 Make a foot-long leader with a size 1 to 2/0 treble hook on one end and a barrel swivel on the other.

2 Push a piece of wire with a sharp bend on the end through the blood bait, hook an eye of the barrel swivel and then pull the leader through the bait.

3 Slide the bait down to the hook and impale it with all 3 points of the treble. Attach the leader to a clip at the end of your line.

INDEX